KU-578-854

The LIBERTY Book of Home Sewing

Text by Lucinda Ganderton

Photography by Kristin Perers
Illustrations by Richard Merritt

Quadrille
PUBLISHING

ARTHUR LASENBY LIBERTY OPENED HIS SHOP ON REGENT STREET IN 1875 SELLING IMPORTED TEXTILES FROM JAPAN, CHINA AND INDIA. During the 1870s the Aesthetic Movement was at its height and the followers of this art movement were Liberty's most important customers. Arthur's ideas chimed with theirs when he wanted to influence the public taste by giving them the opportunity to buy beautiful things that were also affordable.

He therefore quickly started selling more than just textiles, and customers came to him for anything from Japanese fans, screens and wallpapers to blue and white pottery from China, inlaid boxes and wooden carvings from India and Persian metalwork and rugs. Fabrics, however, were the most important part of his stock, and, as soon as he was able to, this is where he began the production of exclusive styles.

He approached Thomas Wardle, the dyer and printer in Leek, Staffordshire, who had earlier collaborated with William Morris on redeveloping vegetable dyes. Wardle created new dyes for Liberty's imported silks which became an instant success and would become known as 'Liberty Art Colours'. These lovely silks in all hues and shades hung in Liberty's windows in Regent Street and were written about in the newspapers of the day. Wardle also developed Liberty's earliest printed designs based on Indian wood-block prints, which were shown at the Paris International Exhibition in 1878.

As this venture became increasingly successful, top designers were commissioned to produce patterns for Liberty. These would be printed or woven by companies in Britain and France and would be promoted as Liberty designs. Arthur Lasenby Liberty was a clever marketing man, and he knew that his name was a very valuable asset. The company went public in 1894 as Liberty & Co Ltd, although the public would always know it as Liberty's. By this time, besides the fabrics, Liberty's were producing their own fashion line, 'art furniture', 'art metal ware' and 'art jewellery'.

Although the fabrics were printed by many different manufacturers, there was one small print works in Merton, on the River Wandle, that had its production line taken over completely by Liberty and in 1904 they bought the business. The mostly silk fabrics were hand-printed using wood blocks. At its height, there would be 52 block printers employed at Merton. A fine paisley shawl would take many hours to complete, with some designs needing up to 27 different blocks. As each block took two weeks to make, it became clear that this method was becoming too expensive and during the 1930s, screen printing was introduced at Merton. This was still a fairly new technique for commercial printers, and it wasn't until after the Second World War that all the most popular block prints were converted to screen. In the early 1960s the block production was finished and people still remember the piles of blocks that were burned outside the print works. A large number of them were sold in the store on Regent Street and some of the most beautiful ones were kept for the archive.

Liberty's during these years had managed to build up a valuable textile archive of pattern books, artwork, fabric samples and print impressions (a printer's test of a design on paper). This archive has always been viewed as an important design resource. It is fascinating to see design history through the textiles in this archive. The Aesthetic style gives way to Art Nouveau, which in Italy is still known as Stile Liberty; a smaller amount of typical Art Deco designs are taken over by the small florals of the 1930s that Liberty's is still famous for today. The 1950s pushed the contemporary style, while the colourful psychedelic 1960s designs move onto the majestic paisleys of the 1970s and the large furnishing florals of the 1980s to the monochrome designs of the early 1990s.

The Merton print works were sold in 1972, and apart from a brief time during the 1980s, Liberty fabrics have been printed out-house ever since. Up until the mid 1990s, Liberty's cottons were mostly printed in Lancashire by copper roller method, a procedure that was able to produce very fine lines. Unfortunately, because of the size of the rollers, the width of the cloth was restricted to approximately 90 centimetres, and it was decided that it would be more commercially viable to convert the production to screen printing. Nearly all Liberty's fabrics are now machine screen-printed using either the flat bed or rotary methods, and recently some designs are printed digitally. Liberty's prints are on many different bases: cottons, man-mades, silks and wools. All the bases are given Liberty names, such as Varuna Wool, Jubilee (cotton/wool mix), Rossmore Cord, Balcombe Silk. The most famous base in the range since the late 1920s is probably their cotton lawn. Liberty's fabric buyer in the 1920s and 30s was William Haynes Dorell, who decided to market this cotton as Tana Lawn, naming it after Lake Tana in Sudan, where the particular cotton plant used for these fine cottons came from.

The production of Liberty fabrics starts in the design studio. The studio works two years ahead (for example, in autumn 2010 they started to design the collection for autumn 2012), and this means that the designers need to keep well ahead of the coming trends. The designers have a different theme for each collection they do. Designs are based on research done in the Liberty archive and each season the studio will also go further afield for their research and inspiration. A number of designs are commissioned from artists and designers outside the business. Each spring and autumn a new fabric range is launched to complement Liberty's classic designs that are not as bound to the seasons. Some of these classic designs, such as 'Elysian', date back to the early twentieth century or even earlier, like 'Lodden', which was designed as a furnishing fabric by William Morris in 1883.

One important aspect of Liberty's textiles has been the colouring. From Thomas Wardle's Liberty Art Colours to today's designs, much emphasis has always been towards getting the colours absolutely right. Printers send their tests to the studio and many designs go back and forth until the studio are satisfied that the colour and the print quality is as good as can be achieved. Some of the designs are easier to print than others; some are fairly straightforward one-colour designs such as 'Capel', but the design 'Vonetta' involved so-called discharge printing, where one of the screens is used to print a form of bleach, instead of a colour, onto the dyed ground to extract that dye. 'Bailando en Mis Suenos' was digitally printed, which is a relatively recent process to commercial printing.

The range of fabrics used in this book has been chosen from both the seasonal and the classic collections. It is therefore no surprise that we will find some that are historical designs such as 'Wiltshire', 'Lodden' and 'Elysian', some are more recently chosen and adapted from the Liberty archive such as 'Kate Nouveau' and 'Lord Paisley', while others are completely new, such as 'Willow's Garden' and 'Explosions in the Sky'. The majority come from two seasons: spring/summer 2011 when the theme was 'The Story Book', a collaboration between the Liberty design studio and a number of book illustrators; and the autumn/winter 2011 theme, which is 'Liberty Rocks', in which the patterns were either inspired by music and art or designed by musicians who had links to the art world and artists who had links to the music world.

The designs show that although Liberty is closely associated with the lovely small floral prints, they also produce some less characteristic designs. Liberty's collections have always had this eclectic element to it, and I believe that it is this, together with the beautiful colouring and the quality of the fabrics that ultimately makes a Liberty Print.

Anna Buruma
Archivist
LIBERTY ART FABRICS

Essentials

Basic Cushions

Cushions don't have to be complicated. Traditional covers made from furnishing fabrics are trimmed with piping, braid or fringes and fastened with concealed zips. None of these are really essential, particularly when you are using fine cotton, like these Liberty Tana Lawns. This assorted batch acts as a great showcase for a mixture of plains and prints, and shows just how well a selection of prints that span three centuries can work together, from William Morris's 'Lodden', designed in 1884, through 'Lord Paisley' from the 1950s to 'Vonetta' launched in 2011.

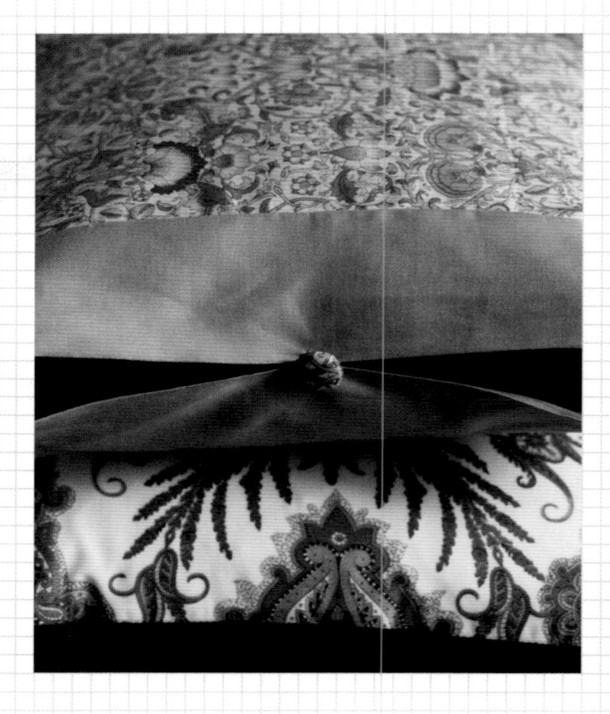

You will need

- Liberty Tana Lawn in a print (or prints), a lightweight cotton fabric, in required amount
- Solid-coloured lightweight cotton fabrics, in required amount
- Matching sewing thread
- Square cushion pad of preferred size

Cutting out

FOR THE BASIC SQUARE CUSHION

FROM PRINT (TANA LAWN IN 'LORD PAISLEY'):

- Cut 1 front panel, the width and depth of filler pad

FROM SOLID-COLOUR:

- Cut 1 back panel, the width and depth of filler pad

FOR THE STRIPED SQUARE CUSHION

FROM TWO PRINTS (TANA LAWN IN 'VONETTA' AND 'LODDEN') AND TWO SOLID-COLOURS:

- Cut 7–9 strips of different widths, the depth of filler pad, to make the front panel

FROM SOLID-COLOUR:

- Cut 1 back panel, the width and depth of filler pad

FOR THE SLIP-ON CUSHION COVER

FROM PRINT (TANA LAWN IN 'LODDEN'):

- Cut 1 main cover piece twice the depth of filler pad and five sixths of the width.

FROM SOLID COLOUR:

- Cut 1 border strip twice the depth of filler pad and one third of the width, plus 2cm

FOR THE WRAPAROUND CUSHION COVER

FROM MAIN PRINT(TANA LAWN IN 'VONETTA'):

- Cut 1 cover piece, two and a half times the width of filler pad and the same depth

FROM BORDER PRINT (TANA LAWN IN 'LODDEN'):

- Cut 1 strip, the depth of filler pad and 6cm wide

FROM SOLID COLOUR:

- Cut 1 strip, the depth of filler pad and 4cm wide
- Cut 1 strip, the depth of filler pad and 12cm wide

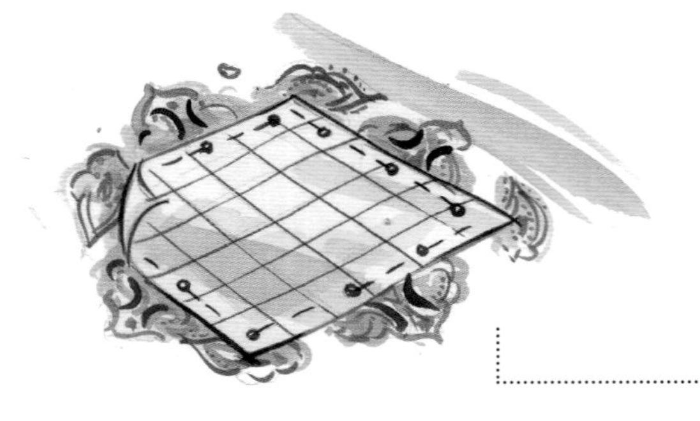

Basic Square Cushion

This entry level cushion cover is not removable, but if you need to launder it, simply unpick the hand-stitched edge and take out the cushion pad. (For a cushion cover back with a simple opening, see Taking it Further on page 17.)

Cutting out the front panel Make a paper pattern piece for your front panel. If you are using a distinctive, large-scale print like 'Lord Paisley', allow extra fabric so you can centre the design exactly within the square template. Pin the pattern piece carefully in place and cut out around the outside edge.

Pinning the front panel to the back Pin the front and back panels around three edges, with right sides together.

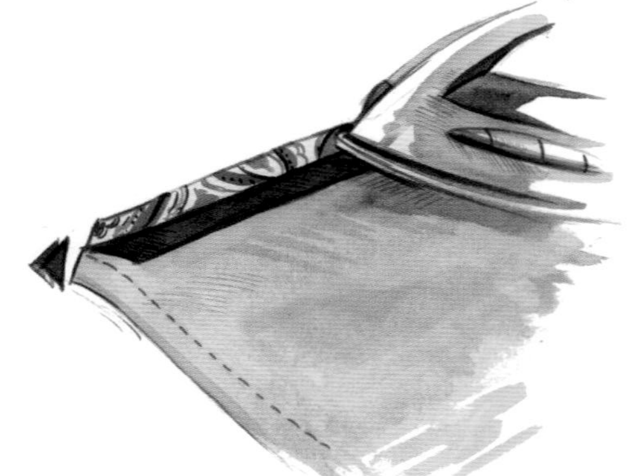

Stitching the front and back together Machine stitch the pinned edges with a 1cm seam. Clip a small triangle from each corner, cutting no closer than 3mm from the stitching. Press back the seam allowances on both sides of the opening, then turn the cover right side out. Ease out the corners and press the seams lightly.

Closing the opening Insert the cushion pad and pin the two sides of the opening together along the folds. Slipstitch the folded edges together as shown on page 153.

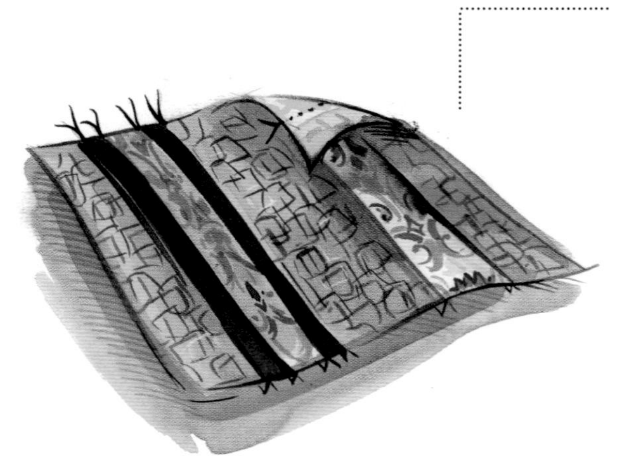

Striped Square Cushion

Make up these simple stripes in an ordered way with a repeating pattern of colours and width, or more randomly, in true patchwork tradition, with scraps saved from other projects.

Making the front panel Machine stitch the lengths of fabric together, with a 1cm seam. Press all the seam allowances towards the darker fabrics and trim to the same size as the back panel.

Finishing the cover Stitch the completed front to the back panel. Insert the cushion pad as for the Basic Square Cushion.

Slip-on Cushion Cover

This open-ended cover goes over a plain basic cushion: mix contrasting plains and florals or darks and lights.

Adding the border Press the border strip in half lengthways and then press under a 1cm turning along one long edge. With right sides together and raw edges aligned, pin the edge of the border without the turned-under seam allowance to the main cover piece. Machine stitch with a 1cm seam and press the seam allowance towards the border.

Stitching the front and back together Unfold the creases and fold the cover in half widthways with right sides together. Matching the crease and seam lines, pin the side and bottom edges together. Machine stitch 1.5cm from the edge. Trim the corners and turn right side out. Ease out the corners and press lightly.

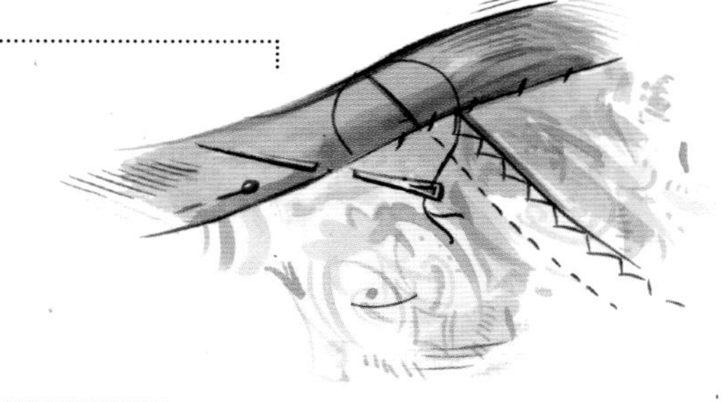

Finishing the cushion Refold the border onto the wrong side of the cover so it conceals the seam allowance. Pin the folded edge to the cushion and slipstitch to the cover. Insert the plain basic cushion. You can leave the opening as it is, or join the two edges with ties or a button.

Taking it further – envelope back

If you want to be able to remove your cushion pad from your basic cushion without having to unstitch a seam – but don't want to have to insert a zip – make an envelope back with two overlapping panels. First decide on the width of the overlap – one third of the width of the cushion is usually about right. Then cut two panel pieces for the back, each half the width of the front cover piece, plus one half the width of the overlap, plus 2cm along the long centre edge for a hem. Machine stitch a 1cm double hem along one long edge of each back panel. Place the completed front panel face upwards and place one back panel along each side edge, with the right sides together and the raw edges aligned. Pin together and machine stitch all around the outside, leaving a 1cm seam. Clip the corners, turn right side out and press. Insert the cushion pad through the back opening.

● THERE ARE NO PRECISE MEASUREMENTS FOR ANY OF THESE COVERS, SO THAT YOU CAN EASILY ADAPT THEM TO FIT ANY SIZE OF SQUARE (OR RECTANGULAR) CUSHION PAD.

Wraparound Cushion Cover

Made from a single piece of fabric with contrasting stripes at one end, this cover has an overlapping opening, like a pillowcase.

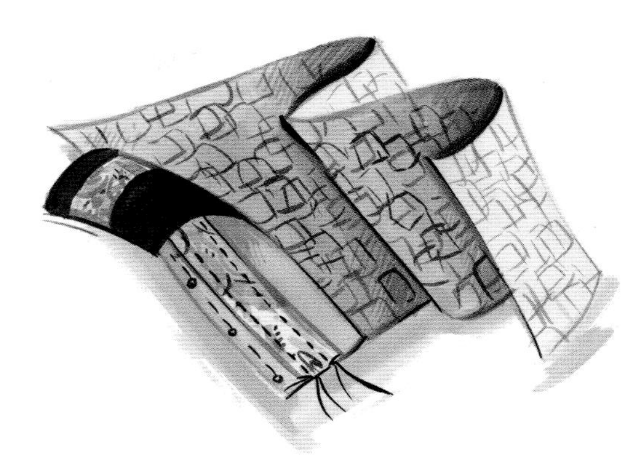

Stitching the border to the cover piece To make the border, machine stitch one solid-coloured strip to each edge of the patterned border strip, with right sides together and leaving a 1cm seam allowance. Press the allowances towards the dark fabric. Pin the narrow solid-coloured strip to one edge of the main cover piece and machine stitch with a 1cm seam. Press the seam allowance towards the border.

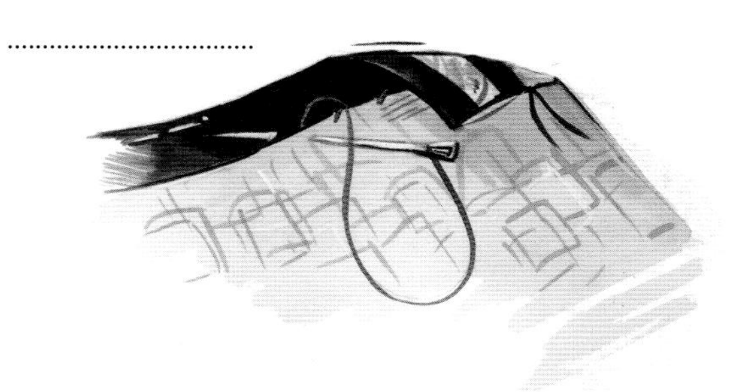

Completing the border Press back a 1cm turning along the edge of the wide solid-coloured strip, then fold it to the wrong side to cover the back of the border. Pin the fold to the main cover along the seam line and slipstitch in place. Press.

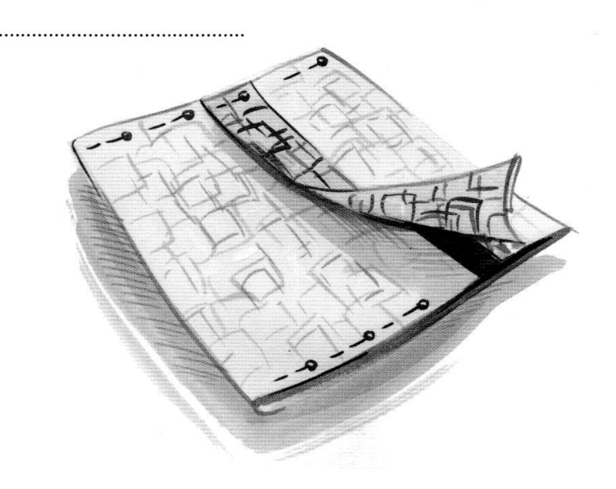

Finishing the cushion Press back a 6cm turning along the other short edge of the main cover piece. Wrap the cover around your cushion pad to work out the best position for the opening: it could be central or to one side. Mark the corners, and remove. Keeping these same corner positions, refold the cover with right sides together, border first. Pin the top and bottom edges together and machine stitch with a 1cm seam. Trim a small triangle from each corner. Turn right side out, ease out the corners and press lightly. Then insert the cushion pad.

● TO GIVE THE CUSHIONS A WELL-FILLED, UPHOLSTERED LOOK, MAKE THE FINISHED COVERS 1CM SMALLER ALL AROUND THAN THE FILLER PAD. CUT THE FRONT AND BACK PANELS TO THE SAME SIZE AS THE FILLER PAD AND USE A 1CM SEAM ALLOWANCE WHEN SEWING THEM TOGETHER.

Simple Curtains

Two billowing lengths of Liberty Tana Lawn make a fabulous pair of sheer curtains. At 136cm, the fabric is wide enough to fit halfway across most windows as a single panel, so all you need to do is hem the edges and add a row of hanging loops. Large-scale print designs, like these 'Viviana' watercolour roses, are shown to full advantage and the fine cotton weave will filter the light, providing privacy whilst still allowing the sun to shine through.

Finished size

A single curtain panel measures 136cm wide by desired drop (see Measuring Up)

You will need

- 136cm wide Liberty Tana Lawn, a lightweight cotton fabric in a large-scale print (see Measuring Up for fabric amounts)
- 25cm of a lightweight white cotton fabric, for header facing
- Matching sewing thread
- Rouleaux maker (optional)

Measuring up

Liberty Tana lawn is 136cm wide: use the whole width for a softly draped effect.

CURTAIN PANEL

width = full width of 136cm wide Tana Lawn

length (drop) = length from bottom of curtain pole to about 5cm from floor, plus 12cm for top and bottom hems (1cm for top turning and 11cm for bottom hem)

CURTAIN LOOPS

allow 13cm extra curtain fabric for making loops for two panels (if making tied loops, allow 30cm extra instead)

Cutting out

FROM PRINT (TANA LAWN IN 'VIVIANA'):

- Cut 2 curtain panels, each 136cm x desired drop (including hems)
- For making loops (for 2 panels), cut 3 narrow strips, each 3.5 x 136cm

FROM WHITE COTTON FABRIC:

- Cut 2 header facings, each 5 x 136cm (if your fabric is narrower than 136cm, piece strips together end-to-end and press seams open to obtain this length)

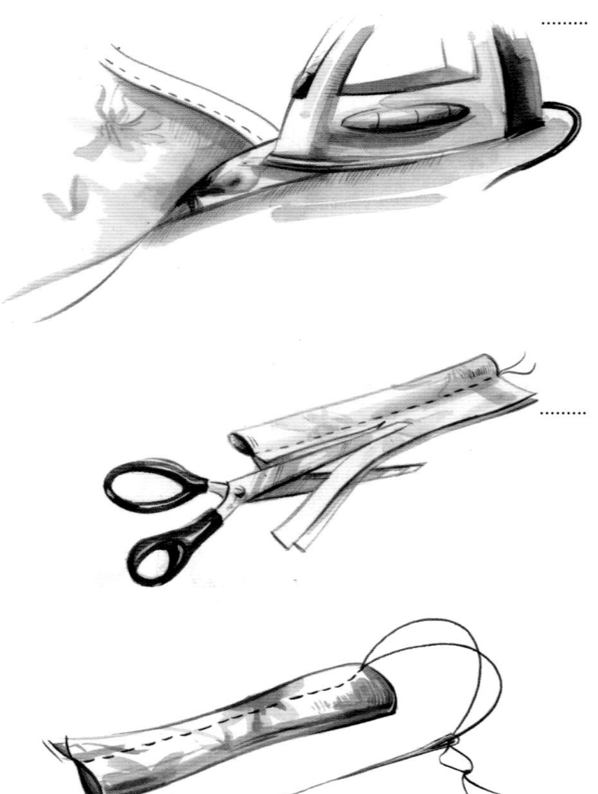

Neatening the side edges Press under a 1cm double hem along each side edge of each curtain panel. Machine stitch using matching sewing thread, then press once again to make sure you have a crisp finish.

Turning up the bottom hem Press a 1cm turning along the lower edge, then press and pin a second turning of 10cm. Use a tape measure or a quilter's ruler to ensure that the hem is the same depth all the way along. Sew the sides and folded edge down by machine with a long straight stitch or by hand with hem stitch.

Making the loops Test that a 18cm finished loop will fit around your curtain pole (adjust this length if necessary, allowing 1cm for a seam allowance at each end). Then, if this length is sufficient, cut 18 lengths of 20cm (nine for each curtain panel) from the three 3.5cm strips of curtain fabric. Fold each strip in half widthways with the right sides facing inwards and machine stitch the long edges together with a 1cm seam. Trim the seam allowance back to 5mm and turn the fabric tube right side out with a safety pin, tapestry needle and thread or a rouleaux maker. Press, so that the seams lie along one edge.

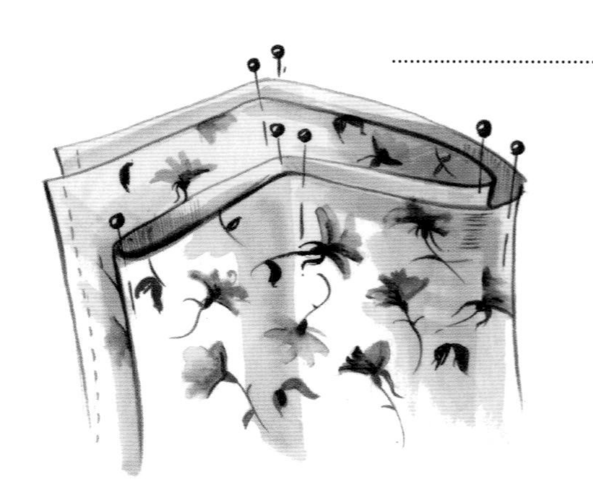

Positioning the loops The quickest way to measure the position of the loops is by simply folding the head of the curtain into eight equal sections. Fold it in half, matching the corners carefully, then into quarters, then into eighths. Mark each fold with a pin. Fold the loops in half, aligning the ends, and pin one to each marker pin position on the right side of the curtain, with the raw edges facing upwards. Pin the remaining two to the corners.

Sewing on the header facing Press under a 1cm turning along the short edges and one long edge of the facing. Pin the unfolded long edge to the top of the curtain, over the loops. Machine stitch 1cm from the raw edge.

Finishing the facing Turn the facing to the wrong side of the curtain. Pin it down and machine stitch around all four edges, 3mm from the fold.

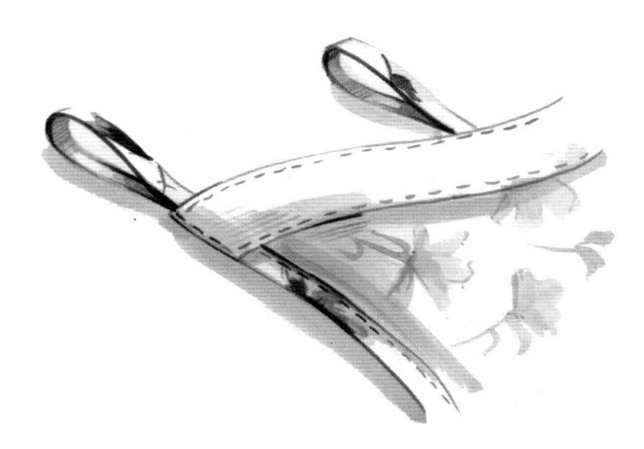

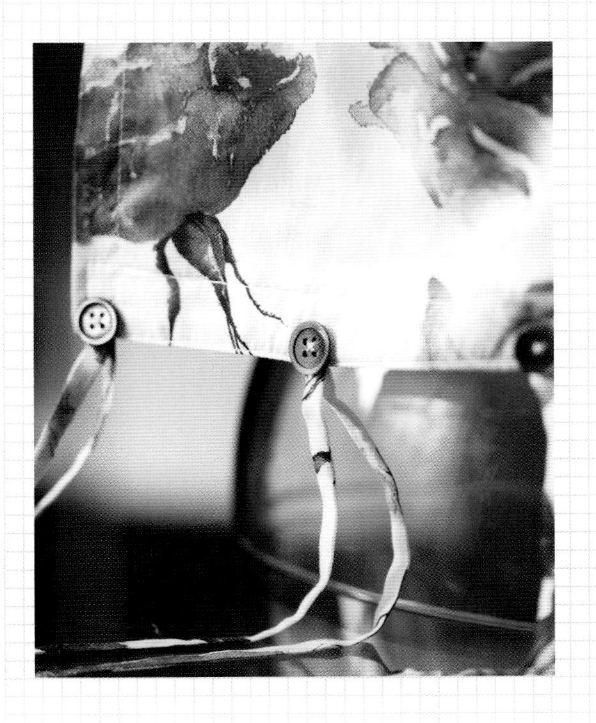

Taking it further – ties

To make ties, instead of loops at the top of the curtains, cut eight 3.5cm wide strips from the fabric (instead of three) for the rouleaux. Then cut 36 lengths from these, each 25cm long, and make 36 rouleaux ties as on page 22. Knot one end of each rouleaux strip and stitch the unknotted ends to the curtain top in pairs. Tie these loose ends around the pole.

● ADD AN EXTRA 30CM TO THE DROP OF YOUR CURTAIN IF YOU WANT IT TO SPILL ONTO THE FLOOR IN SOFT FOLDS.

Eco Shopper

Avoid plastic carriers and maintain your green credentials by keeping an eco-conscious cloth shopper with you at all times. You can make this bag in two practical variations on the same theme: a sturdy and roomy bag in poplin or an equally large fold-away version made from very lightweight Liberty Tana Lawn. The lightweight bag can be folded up and slipped into a tiny bag holder, which you can fix to your handbag or key ring so that you will have no excuses for not using it.

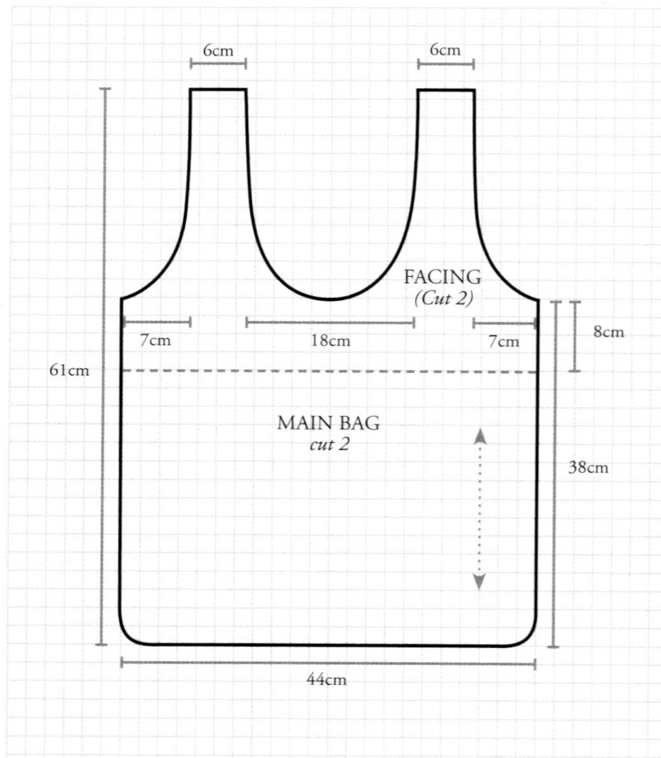

Finished size

- The shopping bag is 42cm wide and measures approximately 36cm from the bottom edge to the handle opening

You will need

- 1m of Liberty Tana Lawn in 'Kayoko' (or poplin), a lightweight (or medium-weight) cotton fabric in a small-scale print
- Matching sewing thread
- Dressmaker's pattern paper
- Key ring fob
- Large press stud

Cutting out

Make a paper pattern for both the main bag piece and the facing piece.

- Cut 2 main bag pieces
- Cut 2 facing pieces (as main bag, but down only to the dotted line)
- Cut 4 bag holder pieces, 10cm x 15cm, and clip off a tiny triangle from each corner of one short edge
- Cut 1 bag-holder loop piece, 4cm x 10cm

Joining the bag pieces together With right sides together, pin the two main bag pieces together around the side and bottom edges. Machine stitch, leaving a 1cm seam allowance. Neaten the seam with a zigzag or overlocking stitch. Turn the bag right side out, ease out the seam and press.

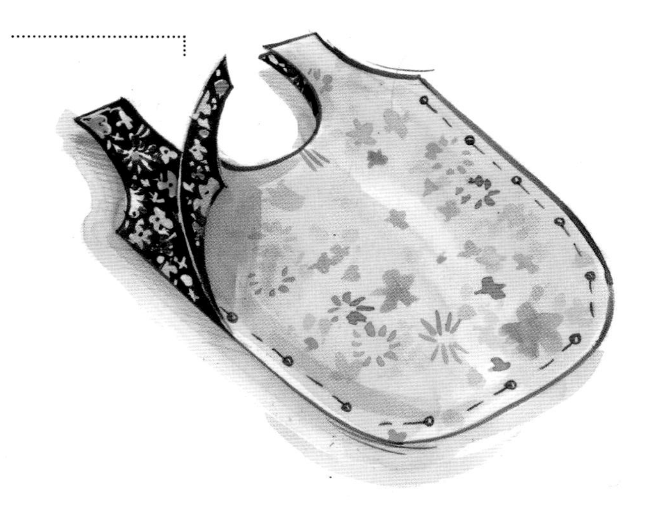

Joining the facing pieces together Again with right sides together, pin the two facing pieces together along the short side edges. Machine stitch 1cm from the edge, then press the seams open.

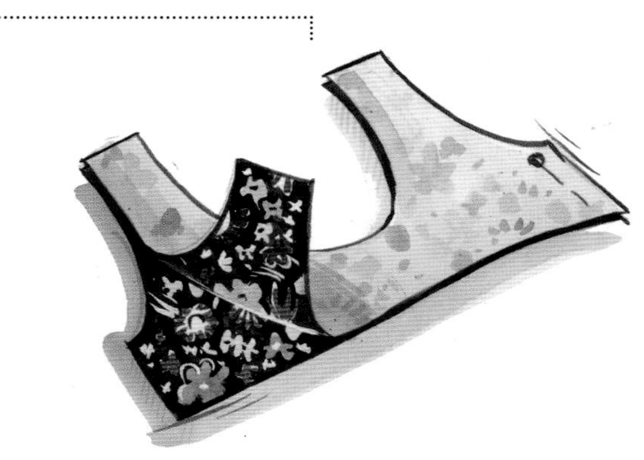

Stitching the facing to the bag Press under and machine stitch a 1cm hem around the bottom edge of the facing. Then slip the prepared facing over the top of the main bag, with the right sides together. Line up the side seams and tops of the handles, then pin the facing to the bag. Machine stitch all the way around the raw edges, leaving a 6mm seam allowance.

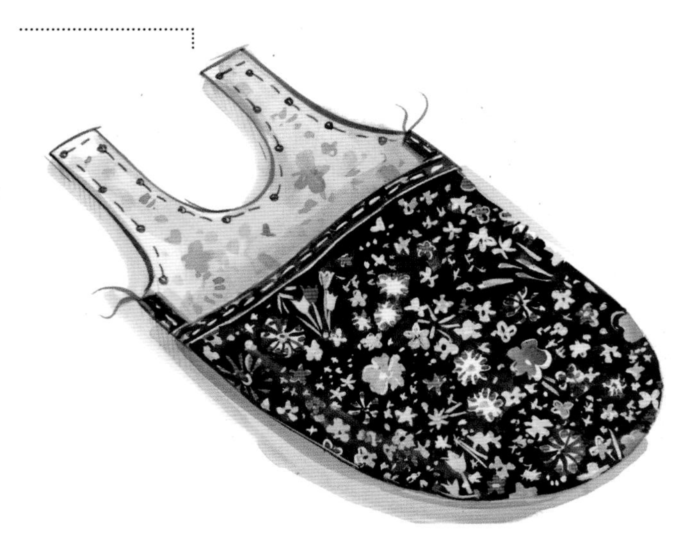

Topstitching along the edge of the handles Trim away a tiny triangle of fabric from each corner of the four handles so that they will lie flat. Now turn the facing right side out so that it is inside the bag. Use a pencil to ease out the corners and roll the seams between your fingers and thumbs so that the stitching lies along the edge. Topstitch all around the top of the bag, 3mm from this edge, then press these seams flat.

Finishing the shopper Pin and tack together the narrow ends of the two handles on the front of the bag, overlapping them by 1.5cm. Sew together with reinforcing stitches: make a strong join by machine stitching a narrow rectangle crossed by two diagonal lines through all four layers. Do the same with the two handles on the back of the bag. Remove the tacking.

● GIVE YOUR BAG A DIFFERENT LOOK BY USING A CONTRASTING OR PLAIN FABRIC FOR THE HANDLE FACING.

Taking it further – bag holder

Preparing the back and front of the bag holder
Pin two bag holder pieces together, with the right sides together, and machine stitch along the two side edges and the shaped top edge, leaving a 6mm seam allowance. Trim the seam allowance back to 3mm all around and turn right side out. Press. Stitch the other two bag holder pieces together in the same way.

Making the bag-holder loop Fold the loop strip in half lengthways with wrong sides together. Unfold, and press in the two side edges so that they line up with the centre crease. Re-fold along the centre fold and press again. Tack together through all four layers. Topstitch along each long edge, 3mm from the outside edge. Remove the tacking.

Stitching the bag holder pieces together Slip the loop through the bottom ring of the key ring and fold it in half. With the raw ends overlapping the bag edge by 2cm, pin and tack the loop to one of the double bag holder pieces, along the raw edges at the bottom of the bag piece. Pin the second bag holder piece on top. Machine stitch around the bottom and two side edges, starting and ending the seam at the angled bottom corners and stitching 3mm from the neatened edges and 6mm from the raw edges. Trim the ends of the loop and turn the right side out so that the key ring projects from the bottom of the bag holder.

Sewing on the press stud Sew one half of the press stud to each side of the opening. Fold up the large shopper tightly, slip it into the holder and close.

• YOU CAN USE A PLAIN SPLIT RING ON THE BAG HOLDER, OR RECYCLE THE METAL PART OF AN OLD KEY RING.

Cook's Apron

Domestic duties demand the protection only a big old-fashioned apron gives. Keep yourself neat and tidy with this practical pinny, which comes with a detachable hand wiper. It's made from from hard-wearing linen, or cotton drill, and trimmed with a wide border of 'Betsy', a charming classic Liberty Tana Lawn. Junior chefs are notoriously messy, and need their own scaled-down aprons to keep themselves clean when at work in the kitchen. The 'Take it Further' option is a reversible apron with a traditional Liberty Tana Lawn on one side and a practical cotton drill on the other. It is remarkably quick to put together and is an ideal first sewing project to make with children.

Finished size

FOR ADULT'S APRON

94cm long from top of bib to hem and 78cm across apron skirt

FOR CHILD'S APRON

50cm long from top of bib to hem and 42cm across apron skirt

You will need

FOR ADULT'S APRON

- For apron, 100 x 100cm piece of an off-white heavy-weight linen or cotton drill
- For ties and borders, 70 x 136cm piece of Liberty Tana Lawn in 'Betsy', a lightweight cotton fabric in a medium-scale print
- Matching sewing thread
- Dressmaker's pattern paper
- Two metal D-rings
- Two 1cm press studs

FOR CHILD'S APRON

- For apron front, 55 x 65cm piece of heavy-weight white cotton drill or calico
- For apron lining, 65 x 65cm piece of Liberty Tana Lawn in 'Betsy', a lightweight cotton fabric in a medium-scale print
- Matching sewing thread
- Dressmaker's pattern paper
- 1.5m of 12mm wide white cotton tape

Making paper pattern pieces

FOR ADULT'S APRON

Make and cut out the paper pattern pieces for the apron and the bib border using the pattern piece diagram. The other six pieces are rectangles, so make these paper patterns using the measurements in Cutting Out on page 32. Cut an angled V-shape at the end of the waist tie and neck loop rectangles, 5cm deep.

FOR CHILD'S APRON

Make paper pattern pieces for the apron and the pocket and use these to cut the fabric pieces.

HOOVER

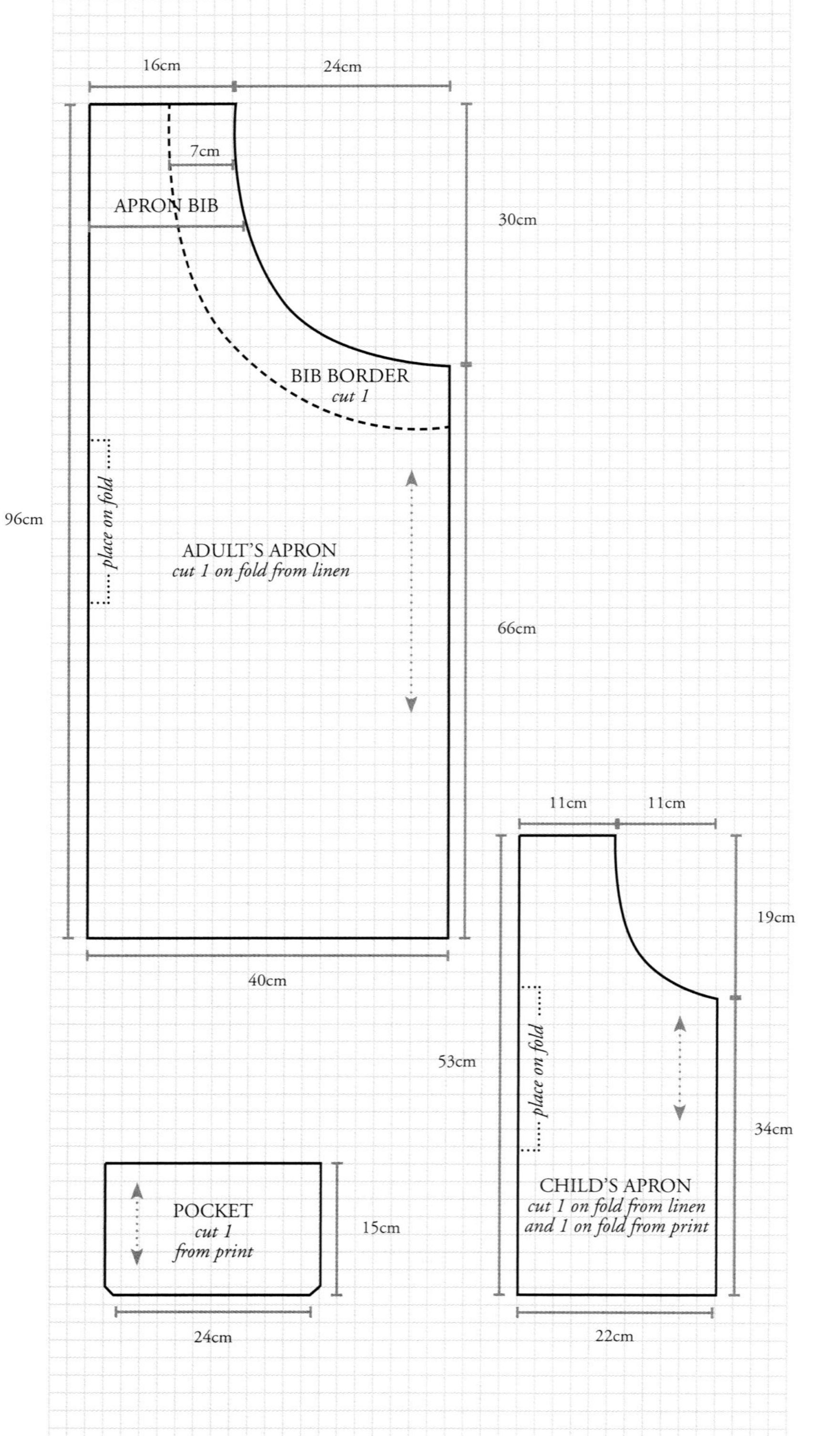

Cutting out

Launder and press the fabrics before cutting out, so that the main apron will not shrink and distort the bindings.

FROM LINEN OR COTTON DRILL:

for adult's apron

- Cut 1 apron piece on the fold
- Cut 1 hand wiper, 35 x 25cm

for child's apron

- Cut 1 apron piece on the fold, for apron front

FROM PRINT:

for adult's apron

- Cut 2 bib borders (one reversed)
- Cut 1 neck border, 7 x 32cm
- Cut 2 side borders, 7 x 66cm
- Cut 1 hem border, 7 x 80cm
- Cut 2 waist ties, 12 x 60cm
- Cut 1 neck loop, 12 x 87cm
- Cut 1 hand wiper, 35 x 25cm

for child's apron

- Cut 1 apron piece on the fold, for apron back
- Cut 1 pocket

Stitching the bib borders to the wrong side of the apron
Turn under 1cm along the outside edge of each bib border and tack in place, easing the fabric gently inwards around the curve. Pin the right side of each bib border to the wrong side of the apron piece. Machine stitch, leaving a 1cm seam allowance.

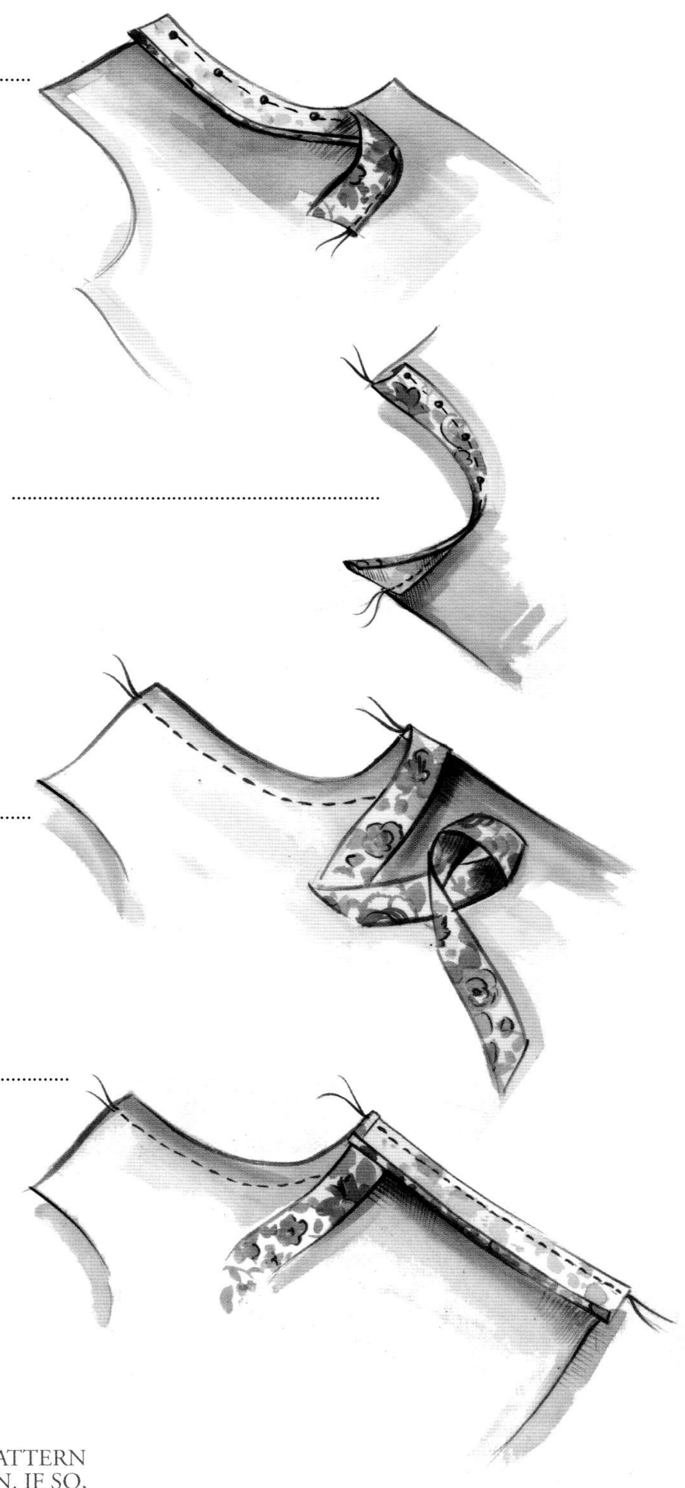

Stitching the bib borders to the right side of the apron
Turn each bib border over to the right side of the bib and press along the curved seam. Pin down the turning and machine stitch to the apron, 3mm from the turning fold. Remove the tacking.

Preparing the waist ties Fold one of the waist tie pieces in half lengthways with right sides together. Pin the long and diagonal edges together, then machine stitch with a 1cm seam. Clip the corner and turn right side out. Ease out the point and press flat. Make the other tie in the same way.

Adding the waist ties Pin the open end of the first waist tie to one armhole corner of the apron on the wrong side, with the folded edge of the tie on top, and machine stitch 6mm from the edge. Stitch the other tie to the opposite corner in the same way.

Stitching the side borders to the apron Press under a 1cm turning along one long edge and the top edge of a side border. With the turnings upwards, pin the long raw edge to one side of the apron on the wrong side, over the end of the waist tie. Machine stitch 1cm from the edge. Turn the border to the front of the apron and pin in place. Machine stitch along the top and long edges, 3mm from the turning fold. Add the second side border in the same way. Trim the bottom end in line with the apron.

● YOU MAY WISH TO ADJUST THE SIZE OF THE PAPER PATTERN TO MAKE A LONGER, SHORTER, OR NARROWER VERSION. IF SO, REMEMBER TO ALTER THE MEASUREMENT OF THE SIDE BINDINGS AND SHORTEN OR LENGTHEN THE LOWER ENDS OF THE BIB BINDINGS ACCORDINGLY.

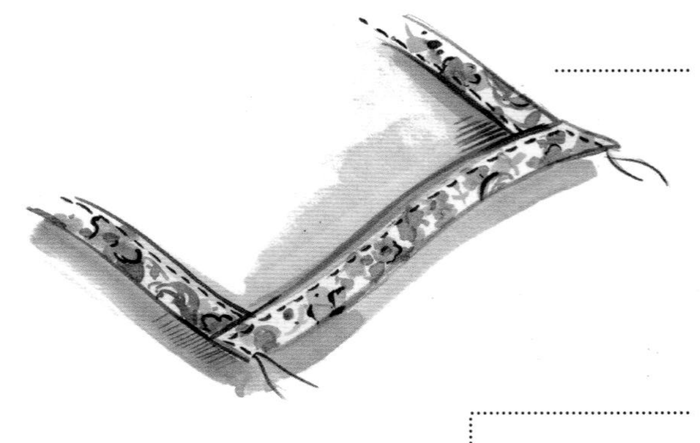

Adding the bottom border Press under a 1cm turning along one long edge and the two short side edges of the border, checking that it fits exactly along the apron hem. Machine stitch it to the apron as for the side borders, then turn it to the right side and stitch in place along the three folded edges 3mm from the turning folds.

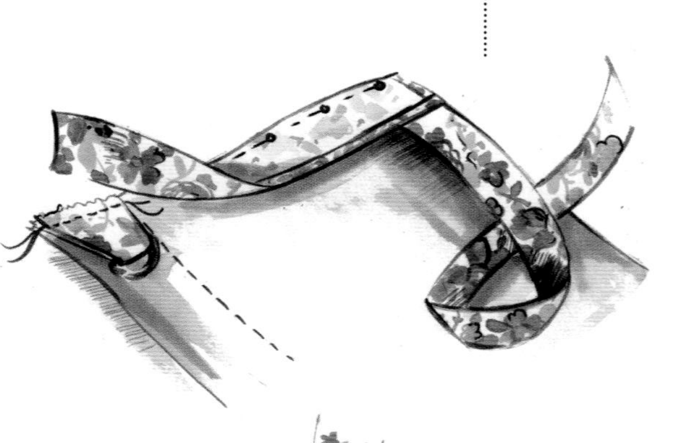

Finishing the neck edge Make up the neck loop as for the side ties, then cut a 10cm length from the open end. Thread this through the two D-rings, fold in half widthways and machine stitch the raw edges to the wrong side of the left corner of the neck, 6mm from the edge. Stitch the open end of the neck loop to the right corner in the same way. Press under a 1cm turning along one long and two short side edges of the neck border, checking that it fits the neck edge exactly. Pin the raw edge to the wrong side of the apron, lining up the corners. Machine stitch with a 1cm seam, then turn to the right side of the apron and complete as for the other borders.

Threading the neck loop onto the D-rings To secure the adjustable neck loop, pass the end of the tie through both D-rings, then back up between them.

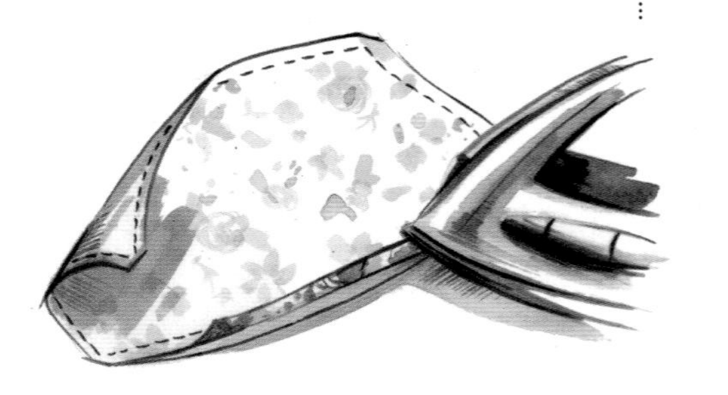

Making the hand wiper With right sides together, pin the two hand wiper pieces together. Machine stitch with a 1cm seam, leaving a 10cm opening along on long edge. Clip the corners, press back the seam allowance on each side of the opening and turn right side out. Ease out the corners and press. Tack the opening together, then stitch all the way round the wiper, 3mm from the edge. Remove the tacking. Fix to the centre of the apron front with two press studs (one in each top corner of the wiper), 13cm lower than the armhole shaping.

Taking it further – child's apron

Preparing the pocket Press under a 1cm turning along each short side and the bottom of the pocket, including the corners. Next, press under 1cm twice along the top edge to form a double hem. Tack these turnings in place. Machine stitch all around the pocket close to the pocket edge, then stitch a second line 6mm from the edge. Remove the tacking.

Adding the pocket Fold the pocket in half widthways and press to mark a vertical line along the centre. Pin it to the centre front of the apron front, 16cm up from the lower edge. Machine stitch around the side and bottom edges, on top of the outer line of stitches. Stitch along the centre crease to divide the pocket into two compartments.

Stitching the back and front together With right sides together, pin the back to the front. Leaving the neck edge open and starting (and ending) 1cm down from the neck edge, machine stitch around the edge, leaving a seam allowance of 1cm. Clip a triangle from each of the side corners, cutting to within 3mm from the seam line. Turn the apron right side out through the neck opening, ease out the corners with the point of your embroidery scissors or a pencil, and press well.

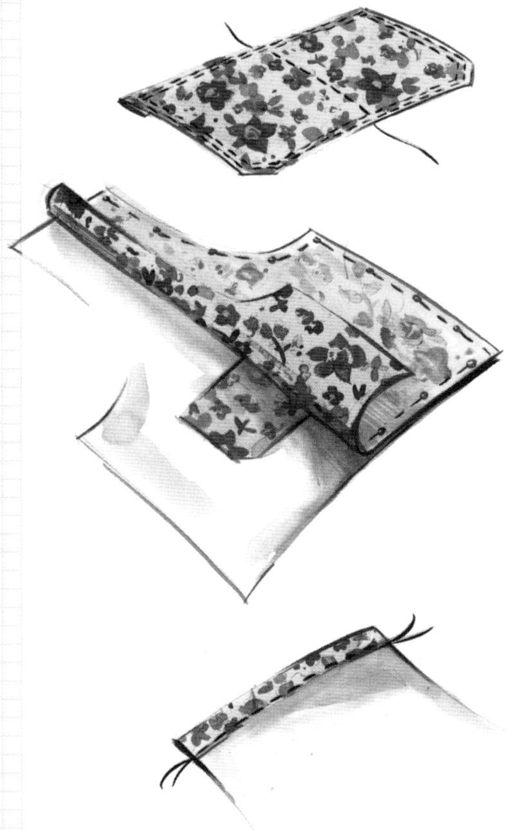

Finishing the neck edge Trim away 1cm of the white apron front along the neck edge, so the fabric print is longer than the white front. Then turn 1cm of the fabric print over to the apron front and press, then press under 1cm of the front and back together. Machine stitch 3mm from the lower fold.

Adding the ties Cut two 50cm lengths of cotton tape and sew one to each side waist corner, on the wrong side of the apron. The remaining tape is used for the neck loop: sew one end to each top corner.

Sugar-Bag Doorstop

Here's a practical solution to an everyday domestic problem. Based on the proportions of a large bag of sugar or flour – and weighing just about the same – this needlecord doorstop is robust enough to keep any door wide open when necessary. It's both functional and stylish, and the granular filling means that nobody will get stubbed toes if they collide with it.

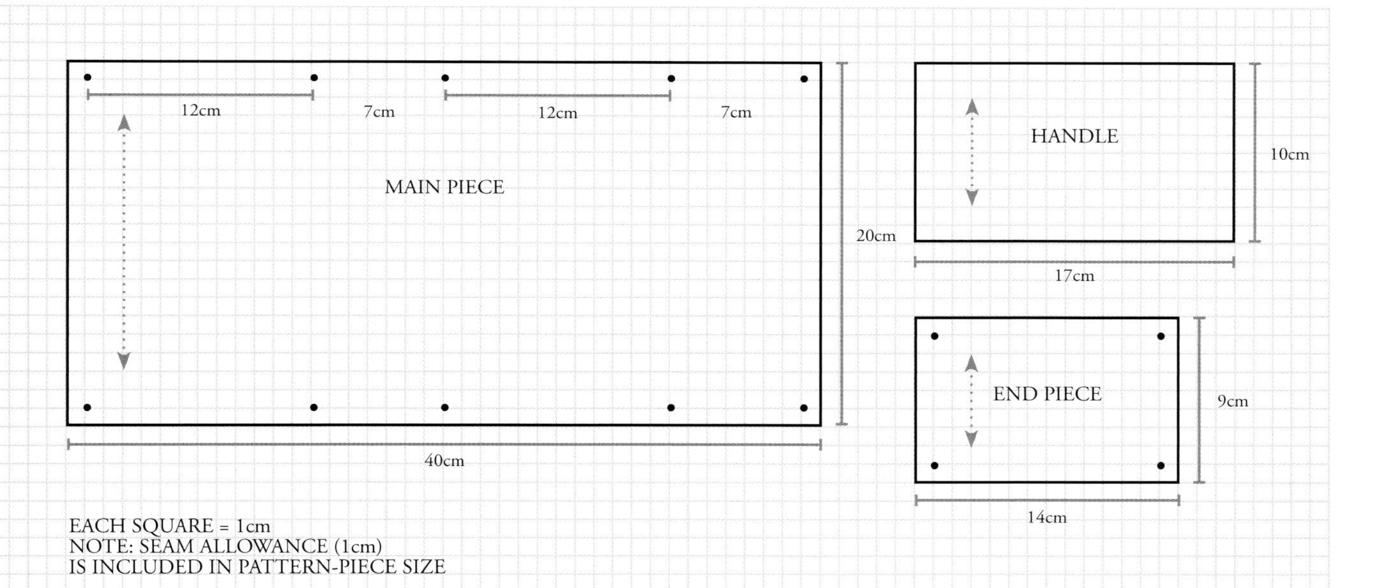

You will need

- 55 x 25cm piece of Liberty Rossmore Cord in 'Mike', a lightweight fine-ribbed corduroy (needlecord) in a broken stripe
- 35 x 25cm piece of co-ordinating plain cotton fabric
- Matching sewing thread
- Cardboard tube (optional)
- Approximately 1.5kg of filling (see tip on page 38)

Finished size

- 18cm tall by 12cm wide by 7cm deep

Cutting out

FROM NEEDLECORD:

- Cut 1 main piece and 1 end piece

FROM PLAIN COTTON:

- Cut 1 handle and 2 end pieces

NOTE: Transfer all the dot markings onto the fabric.

Preparing the handle Press the fabric handle piece in half lengthways with right sides together. Open out the centre crease, then press back a 1cm turning along each long edge. Pin and tack the folded edges together. With matching sewing thread, machine stitch round all around the handle, 3mm from the outside edge. Remove the tacking.

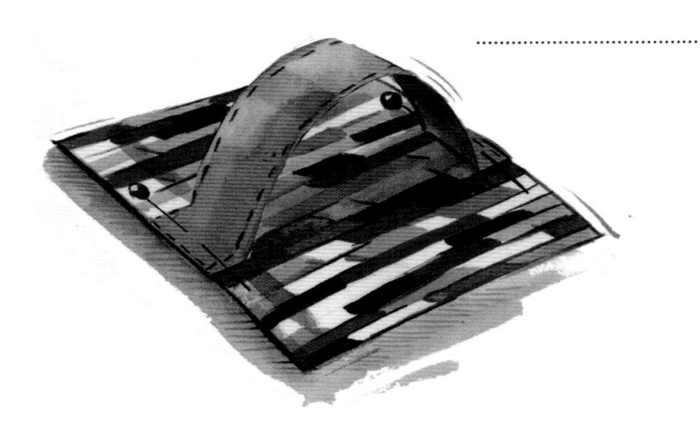

Joining the handle to the end piece Pin the short ends of the handle to the centre of the short edges of the right side of the needlecord end piece, aligning the raw edges. This will be the top of the doorstop. Machine stitch two or three times over both ends of the handle, 6mm from the edge, to make a strong join.

Stitching the main piece to form a cylinder At the ten points indicated on the pattern, make 6mm cuts into seam allowances along the two long edges of the main piece. With right sides together, pin the short edges of the main piece together to make a cylinder. Machine stitch with a 1cm seam allowance, leaving a 1cm length unstitched at each end. Press the seam open.

● IF YOU ARE ALWAYS GOING TO KEEP YOUR DOORSTOP INDOORS, YOU CAN FILL IT WITH RICE, LENTILS OR WHEAT, AND ADD A HANDFUL OF DRIED LAVENDER FOR A SUBTLE FRAGRANCE. HOWEVER A NATURAL FILLING WILL MOULDER IF IT GETS DAMP, SO USE PLASTIC GRANULES INSTEAD IF THE STOP IS INTENDED FOR A FRONT OR BACK DOOR.

Joining the top to the main piece With right sides together and the handle facing inwards, pin the top piece to one open end of the cylinder, matching the dots. The cuts will splay open so that the side piece takes on a rectangular shape. Tack the pieces together, 1cm from the edge, then machine stitch twice around this line. Work two extra rows of stitching along the end of the handles to reinforce the join. Remove the tacking.

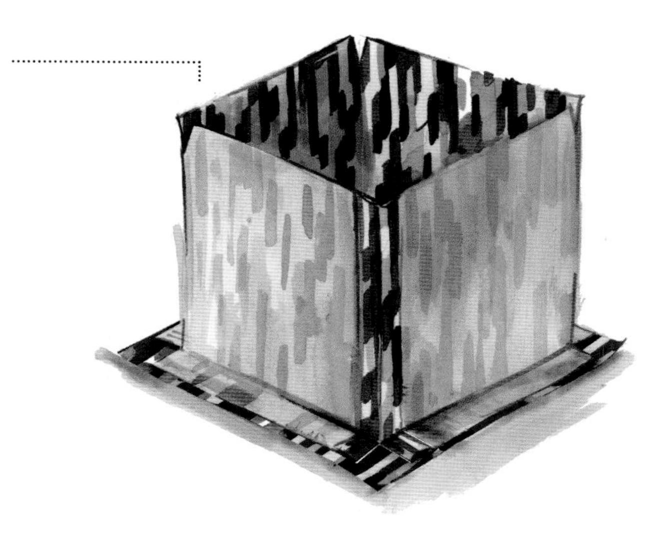

Joining the bottom to the main piece Tack the two plain cotton end pieces together to make a reinforced base. Pin, tack and machine stitch the base to the other end of the cylinder in the same way, leaving an 8cm opening in one long side for filling. Remove the tacking. Then carefully turn the doorstop right side out through the opening – this will be a bit of a struggle, but it is possible. Use a blunt pencil to ease out the corners.

Finishing the doorstop Now it's time to fill the doorstop. The easiest way to do this is to insert a cardboard tube (or a rolled-up sheet of thin cardboard) through the opening and to slowly pour the filling through the top end. Continue until the bag feels completely solid, which may take longer than you expect. Pin the two sides of the opening together. Thread a needle with a double length of thread and neatly and securely hand sew the opening closed, using slipstitch (see page 153).

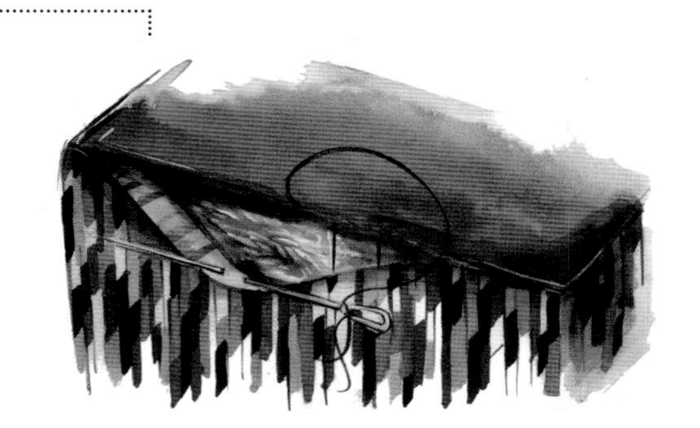

Washbag

Nobody really needs to stitch their own washbag, when there are so many readily available in the stores, at every level from budget to luxury – but who could possibly resist one of these hand-stitched offerings? Filled with carefully chosen toiletries it would make a very special present, or if you're feeling indulgent, sew one for yourself in your favourite Liberty Tana Lawn.

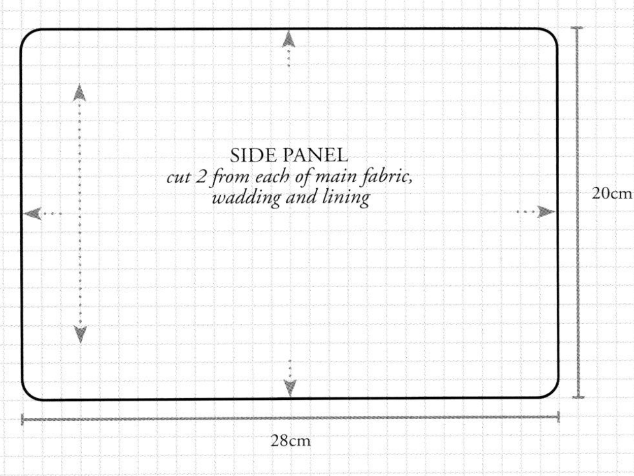

EACH SQUARE = 1cm
NOTE: SEAM ALLOWANCE IS INCLUDED IN CUTTING SIZE

Finished size

26cm wide by 18cm tall by 8cm deep

You will need

- For main fabric, 35 x 110cm piece of Liberty Tana Lawn in 'Sheona' or 'Ameila Star', a lightweight cotton fabric in a medium-scale print
- For lining, piece of lightweight waterproof fabric same size as main fabric
- Lightweight cotton quilt wadding, same size as main fabric
- 42cm plastic zip
- Matching sewing thread
- Dressmaker's pattern paper
- Wire cutters, small pliers and 8mm metal split ring
- Scrap of leather

Making paper pattern pieces

Draw the pattern pieces on dressmaker's pattern paper.

BAG PANEL PIECE

- Add arrows to mark centre point on sides as shown

TOP GUSSET PIECE

- Draw a rectangle 5 x 44cm

BOTTOM GUSSET PIECE

- Draw a rectangle 10 x 53cm

Cutting out

Each of the five bag pieces – two bag side panels, one bottom gusset, and two top gussets – is a three-layered sandwich made up of main fabric, batting, and a lining. For each of the five pieces, cut a rectangular three-layered sandwich as explained on page 42.

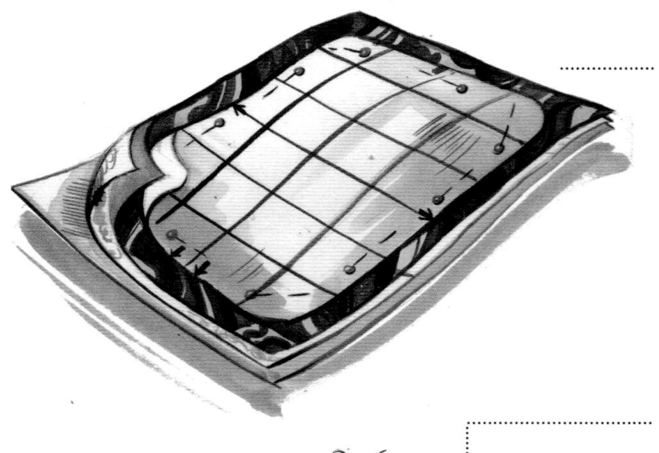

Preparing the five layered pieces of the bag Prepare the layers for each of the five bag pieces (see Cutting Out), by cutting a piece of each of the three layers about 2cm larger all around than the paper pattern piece. Stack them together with the lining face down at the bottom, then the wadding and the main fabric – right side up – on top. Pin the pattern piece through all three layers. Machine stitch them together, following the edge of the pattern exactly. Trim the seam allowance down to 3mm and transfer any pattern markings.

Stitching the zip to a top gusset piece Open the zip. Place one straight edge along the right side of the long edge of a top gusset piece so that the bottom end of the zip lies about 1.5cm in from the edge. If necessary, allow the top end of the zip to overlap the gusset – you can stitch through the extra length and trim it later. Tack the zip tape in place. Fit a zip foot to your machine and stitch 3mm from the teeth. When you get half way along, lift up the foot, leaving the needle in the down position. Close the zip, and continue stitching to the end.

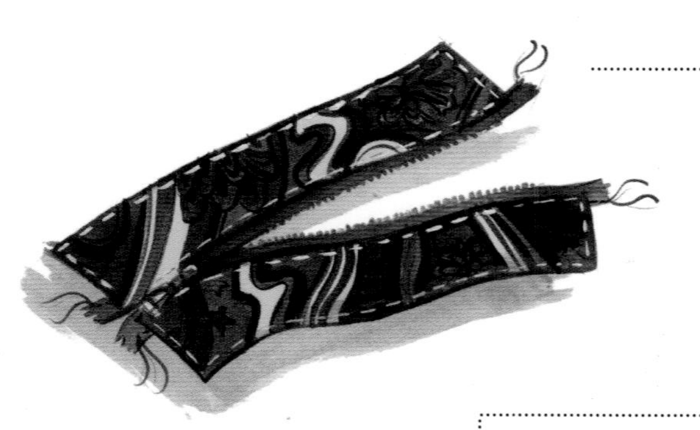

Stitching the zip to the other top gusset piece Press the zip tape to the wrong side and topstitch to anchor down the tape, 3mm from the seam. Sew the other top gusset piece to the second side of the zip in the same way. Remove the tacking.

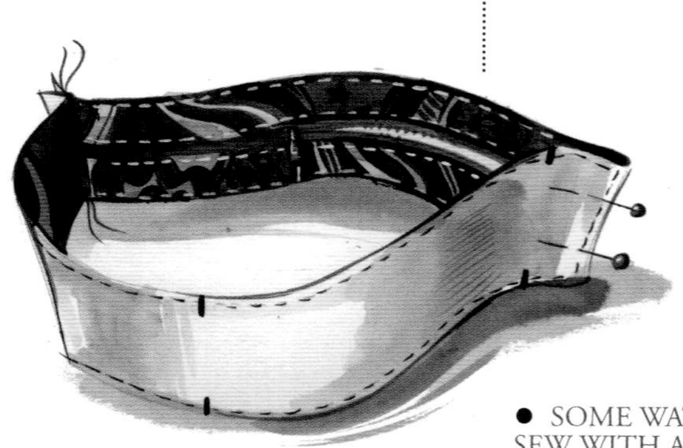

Making the gusset If necessary trim the width of the top gusset piece to the same width as the bottom gusset piece. Then with right sides together, pin the short ends of the top and bottom gusset pieces together to form a loop. Line up the two open ends of the top gusset. Machine stitch with a 1.5cm seam. On the wrong side, mark the centre of the top gusset and the centre of the bottom gusset, then the centre on both sides between these points (these are to match to the centre marks on the side panels).

• SOME WATERPROOF OR PLASTICISED FABRICS ARE DIFFICULT TO SEW WITH AND REQUIRE A SPECIAL PRESSER FOOT FOR THE SEWING MACHINE. A LIGHTWEIGHT FABRIC DESIGNED FOR MAKING SHOWER CURTAINS IS A GOOD OPTION AS IT IS EASY TO CUT AND SHOULD WITHSTAND ALL BUT THE MESSIEST OF SPILLS.

Topstitching the gusset seam Press the seam allowances away from the zip and topstitch 3mm from the seam.

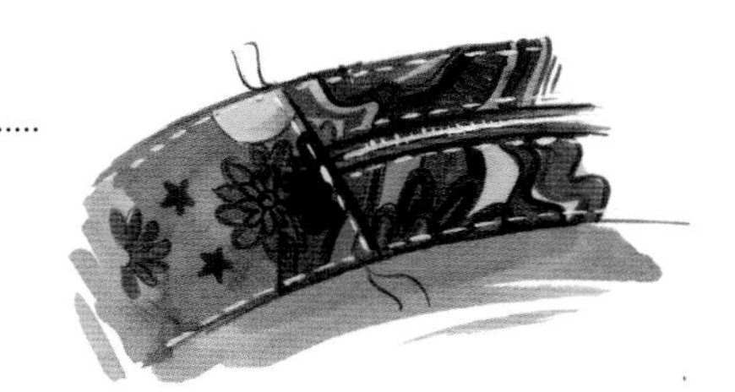

Pinning on the side panels With right sides together, pin one side piece to the gusset loop, matching the centre points at all four edges. Pin out towards the corners on each side, until you reach the curve. Make five 6mm snips into the seam allowance of the gusset, so that it will splay out to fit around the corner.

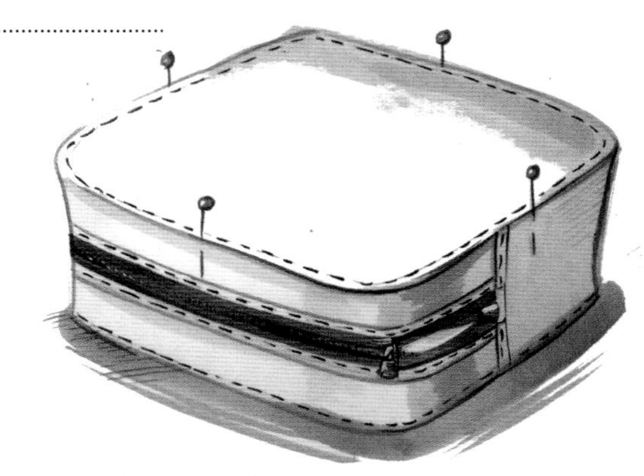

Stitching the side panels to the gusset Tack the two pieces together 1cm from the edge, easing out the gusset to fit the curved corners. Machine stitch all around the side panel, with a 12mm seam. Open up the zip and attach the other side piece in the same way. Neaten the seams with a zigzag or overlock stitch (or bind them if you have the time). Remove the tacking and turn right side out.

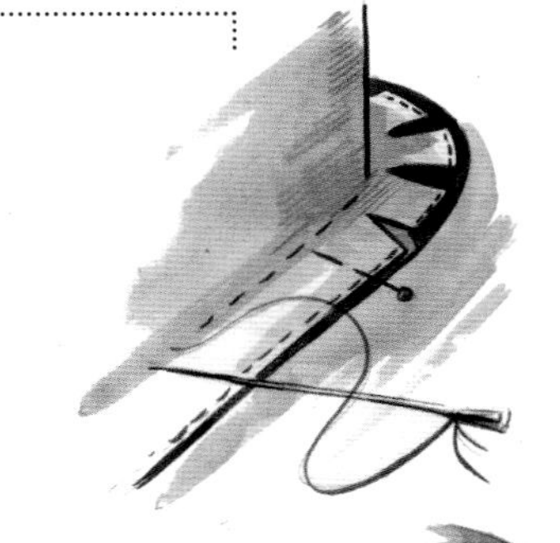

Making the leather zip pull Carefully snip off the metal zip pull with wire cutters. Cut a template from paper in the shape shown below – 7cm long by 2cm wide (across the widest section) and narrow enough at the top end to fit through the split ring. Glue it to one end of the leather scrap. Cut out around the side and bottom edges.

Finishing the leather zip pull Fold the leather pull over and glue to the other end of the leather. Open the split ring with pliers and slip it through the fold. Cut out the leather pull, pass the ring through the zip pull loop and close with the pliers.

Roman Blind

Making a traditional Roman blind can prove a complicated process, involving detailed mathematics, a little basic carpentry and some advanced machine stitching techniques. Here's a quicker, less formal way of sewing an unlined blind that shows off the monochrome design and flowing Art Nouveau lines of this 'Kate Nouveau' canvas print to full advantage, and which can be completed in an afternoon. All the hardware needed can be found at good furnishing suppliers or online.

Finished size

Adjustable to fit your window

You will need

- Liberty Cotton Canvas in 'Kate Nouveau', a heavy-weight cotton furnishing fabric in a large-scale print
- Matching sewing thread
- Sewing kit (sewing machine is optional)
- Dressmaker's pattern paper
- 3cm square wooden batten, same width as blind
- Staple gun
- Thin 3cm wide wooden lath, 3cm shorter than width of blind
- Small blind rings
- Four small screw eyes
- Fine nylon blind cord, 8 times length of blind
- Blind acorn pull
- Large wall screws, wall anchor plugs and 3cm angle brackets to fix wooden batten to wall
- Metal cleat, to wrap cords around when blind is pulled up

Measuring up

The blind hangs from a 3cm square wooden batten, so first of all you need to decide where this is to be fixed. Depending on the size and shape of your window, it can be screwed into the wall above a recessed window, to the top edge of a casement or sash surround or, as here, across the frame that the blind covers just the lower half of the window.

width = width of recess or width of window, plus 15cm for overlap and side hems

length (drop) = distance from top of frame to sill, plus 10cm to cover the wooden batten and make the lath casing – add another 10cm if it the blind is to go outside a recess

Cutting out

Cut out a paper template, taping sheets of pattern paper together as necessary to get the right size. Fold under the allowances and double check the size against your window before you start cutting out, to avoid any errors. Now fold the paper in half widthways. Position the crease along the centre of the fabric, so that the design will be symmetrical across the blind. Pin one half of the paper to the fabric, then unfold the paper, pin down the other half and cut out.

Neatening the side edges of the fabric Make a narrow double hem along each side edge of the blind. Press under a 1cm turning, then a 1.5cm turning, and stitch down the fold by hand or machine.

Making the lath casing The hem of the blind is weighted with a narrow strip of wood, or lath, so that it hangs properly. To make the casing for this, press a 1cm turning along the bottom edge. Press a second 4cm turning and stitch the fold to the blind, by hand or machine. Slide the lath into the casing and slipstitch the side openings closed to keep it in place.

● IF YOU POSITION EACH HORIZONTAL ROW OF RINGS AT THE SAME POINT ON THE PATTERN REPEAT, THE FABRIC WILL FOLD TO CREATE SUBTLY REPEATING SHAPES WHEN THE BLIND IS DRAWN UP.

Attaching the wooden batten Paint the wooden batten to match the fabric or wall if you wish. Screw a metal angle bracket 2cm from each end on the underside (check this distance against your window and adjust as necessary to fit the frame). Place the batten across the top of the blind, on the wrong side with the front edge lying downwards. Staple the edge of the fabric along the back of the batten, half way down: this side will lie against the wall.

Marking the ring positions When the cords are drawn up the blind will fold into soft pleats. The depth of these pleats depends on the distance between the rings that hold the cord: the closer together they are, the smaller the pleat. The rings on this bathroom blind are 15cm apart, but you can increase this distance to create larger folds. Lay a tape measure along the centre of the blind, on the wrong side. Using a disappearing-ink pen, mark the position of the first ring 10cm up from the hem. Mark a series of points along the same vertical line, 15cm (or more) apart. The other two rows of rings lie 5cm from the side edges, and at the same intervals.

Adding the screw eyes Fix three screw eyes into the underside of the batten in line with the rows of rings. Decide which side you want the pull cord to hang; fix the fourth screw eye into this end of the batten, 2cm from the end.

Threading the cords Tie one end of the cord securely to the bottom ring on the pull cord side. Thread the other end up through the rings and the two screw eyes, then out to the side. Cut it 20cm below the hem. Thread the second and third cords in the same way, taking the ends through the screw eyes and cutting them to the same length. Thread the ends of the cord through the blind acorn pull and knot them loosely.

Hanging the blind Fix the blind on the window frame with the angle brackets or by screwing the batten directly into the wall, 10cm above the recess. Adjust the cords to the same length and the blind pull hangs in line with the hem. Knot securely and trim the ends.

Attaching the metal cleat Screw the metal cleat to the wall or window, and wind the cords around it when the blind is drawn up.

Beanbag

Whether you prefer to call this a pouffe, a footstool or an ottoman, it's guaranteed to prove a highly versatile addition to your living space. You can put your feet up on it, pile it high with books and magazines or use it for additional seating – although it's likely to be commandeered by small children and pets as the most comfortable place to curl up and rest. The beanbag is covered in Liberty Rossmore Cord, which is soft to the touch and slightly stretchy, giving a pleasingly plump and upholstered look.

Finished size

40cm in diameter by 30cm deep

You will need

- For main fabric, 90 x 136cm piece of Liberty Rossmore Cord in 'Pablo Pepper', a soft, lightweight, fine-ribbed corduroy in a mini print
- For base fabric, 45 x 50cm piece of of a heavy-weight calico
- For liner fabric, 90 x 136cm piece of a lightweight cotton fabric or lightweight calico
- Dressmaker's pattern paper
- 40cm zip
- Matching sewing thread
- Polystyrene beads to fill liner (56 litres were used here)

Cutting out

FROM MAIN FABRIC:

- Cut 1 top piece, using circular top pattern piece
- Cut 1 sides piece, 32 x 136cm
- Cut 2 handle pieces, each 16 x 18cm

FROM BASE FABRIC:

- Cut 2 base pieces, using base pattern piece

FROM LINER FABRIC:

- Cut 2 top pieces, using circular top pattern piece
- Cut 1 sides piece, 32 x 136cm

NOTE: Seam allowance is included in cutting size.

Making paper pattern pieces

TOP PATTERN PIECE

- Draw a 42cm circle for the top on dressmaker's pattern paper and cut out the shape.
- Fold the pattern piece for the top in half and draw around it on dressmaker's pattern paper, then add 2cm along the straight edge for the opening turnbacks. Cut out the piece.

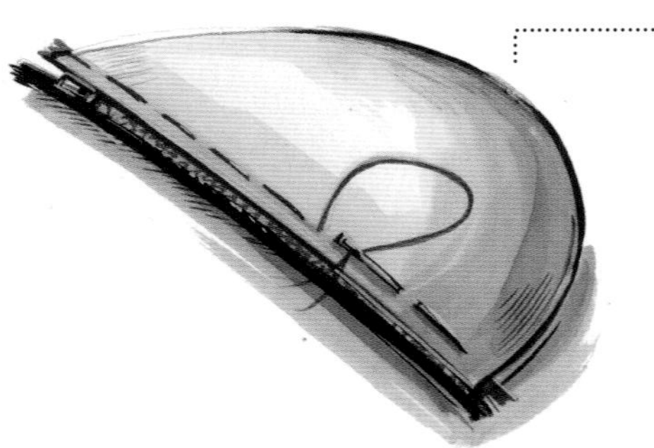

Making the base Press under a 2cm turning along the straight edges of the base pieces. Open out the zip and tack the zip tape below the first base piece, so that the teeth lie against the folded edge. Tack the second base piece to the other side in the same way. Fit a zipper foot to your sewing machine and stitch 3mm from the teeth on each side. Remove the tacking.

Making the handles Press the handle pieces in half lengthways with wrong sides together. Then unfold, turn the raw edges to the centre and press. Press under 1cm at each end. Refold in half and machine stitch 3mm from each long edge.

Seaming the side piece With right sides together, pin together the two short ends of the large sides piece to make a cylinder. Machine stitch, leaving a 1cm seam allowance. Press the seam open and turn right side out.

Adding the handles Pin one of the handles centrally across the seam on the sides piece, 12cm down from the top edge. Sew the ends down with reinforced stitches: a small rectangle with two diagonal lines across the centre. Sew the other handle to the opposite side in the corresponding position.

- ADJUST THE MEASUREMENTS IF YOU WANT A LARGER, MORE SEAT-LIKE BEANBAG. YOU CAN BUY LARGE LINERS AND LOOSE BEADS FROM UPHOLSTERY SUPPLIERS.

Marking the pinning points You now need to divide both the circumference of the circle and the top edge of the sides piece into eight equal sections, prior to pinning them together. Fold the top in half, then quarters, then eighths, and mark each fold with a pin. Turn the sides piece wrong side out and do the same on this cylinder.

Stitching the top to the sides piece With right sides together, match the pins on the top and sides and pin the two together at these eight points. Tack the two together, 1cm from the edge. Ease the fabric in each of the two sections so that it is the same length, as you go, making tiny pleats in the sides piece as necessary. Machine stitch, leaving a 1cm seam allowance. Remove the tacking.

Stitching the base to the sides piece Make a series of 6mm snips into the circumference of the base at 3cm intervals, so that it will fit within the side piece. (You don't have to do this for the top as the corduroy has more 'give' than the calico). Stitch on the base in the same way, remembering to half open the zip before you tack it in place. Turn right side out through the opening and press the seams lightly. Fully open the zip.

Making the liner Machine stitch the short edges of the calico side piece together with a 1cm seam, leaving a 10cm opening in the centre. Sew on the circular top and bottom as for the beanbag cover, then turn the liner right side out through the opening. Snip one corner from the bag of beads and carefully push a cardboard tube through the hole and tape it securely in place. Push the other end of the cardboard tube through the liner opening and carefully pour the beads into the liner. Slipstitch the opening closed when the bag is full. Insert the bead-filled liner into the cover – this might involve a bit of wrestling – and close the zip.

Taking it further – patch pocket

A large patch pocket on each side of the beanbag, instead of handles, would make a handy place to store your current paperback, or the remote control unit.

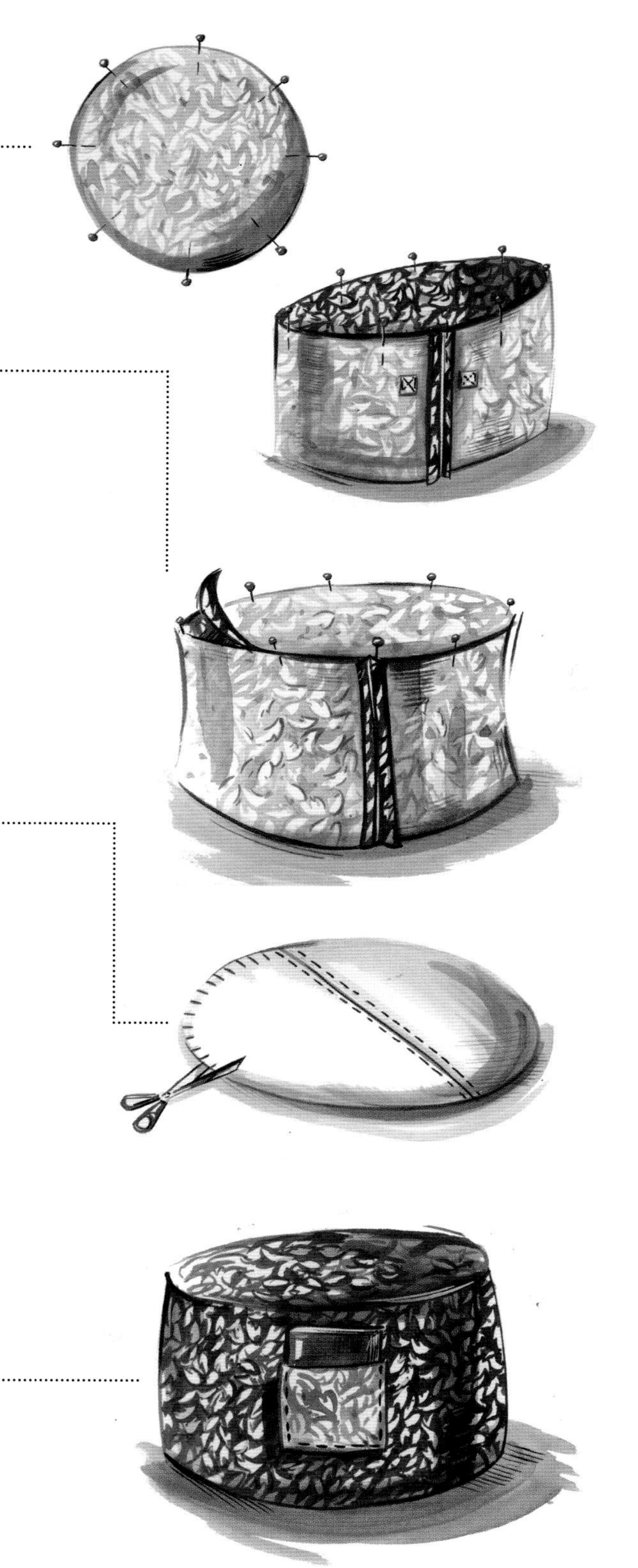

Tote Bag

The unwritten law of accessories dictates that no girl can ever, ever have too many bags; and although the shops are full of desirable handbags, shoulder bags, clutches and totes, there is something really special about making a one-off original that is all your own. Take inspiration from this roomy shopper, which is made from a sturdy cotton canvas in splashy 'Rumble' and lined with an unexpected black and white Tana Lawn 'Millie'.

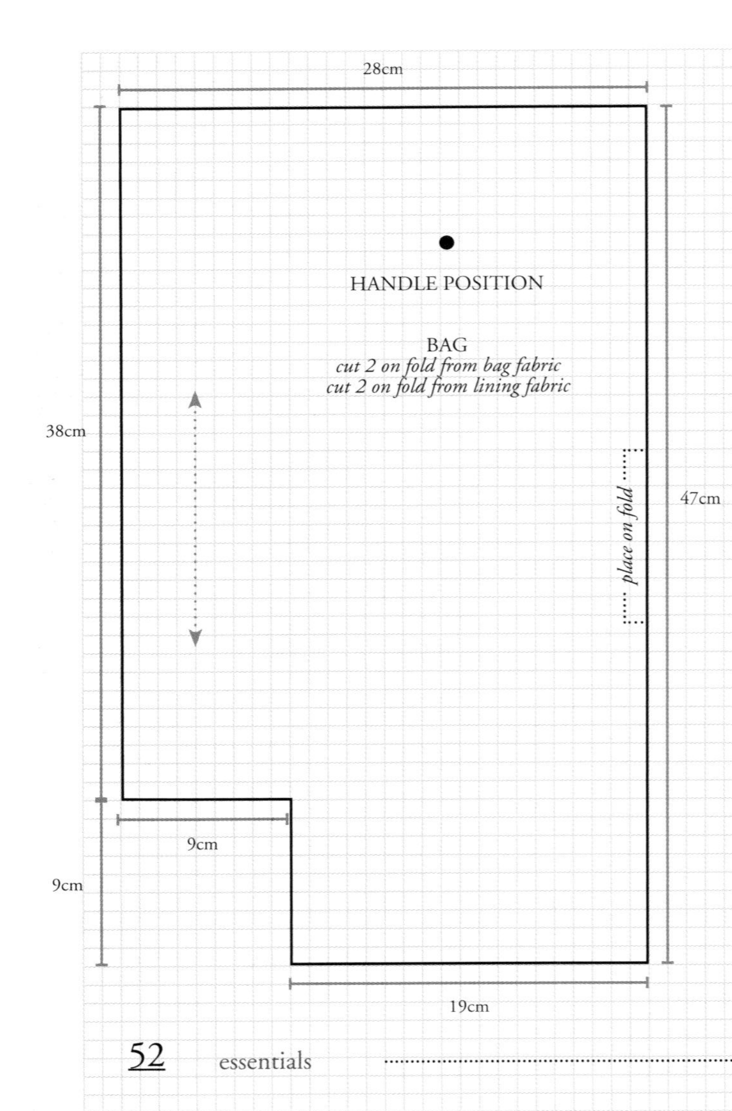

Finished size

- 33.5cm tall (from base) and 53cm wide (from side seam to side seam)

You will need

- For bag, 50cm of 136cm wide Liberty Cotton Canvas in 'Rumble', a heavy-weight cotton furnishing fabric in a print
- For lining, 50cm of Liberty Tana Lawn in 'Millie', a lightweight cotton fabric in a print
- 50 x 112cm piece of medium- or heavy-weight iron-on interfacing (adhesive on one side) to stiffen bag
- Matching sewing thread
- Leather bag handles
- Double-sided cellophane tape
- Quilting thread, for sewing on handles
- Thick cardboard, to stiffen bag base (optional)
- Two 28mm metal bag press studs (optional)

Cutting out

Fuse interfacing to fabric before cutting out bag pieces; cut pocket from area without interfacing.

FROM BAG FABRIC:

- Cut 2 bag pieces on the fold
- Cut 1 pocket piece, 20 x 15cm

FROM LINING FABRIC:

- Cut 2 bag pieces on the fold

EACH SQUARE = 1cm
NOTE: SEAM ALLOWANCE (1.5cm) IS INCLUDED IN PATTERN-PIECE SIZE

GAUDÍ
TASCHEN
PAUL HIMMEL
PHOTOGRAPHS

Pinning the two bag pieces together With right sides together, pin the side and bottom edges of the two bag pieces together, leaving the bottom corners open.

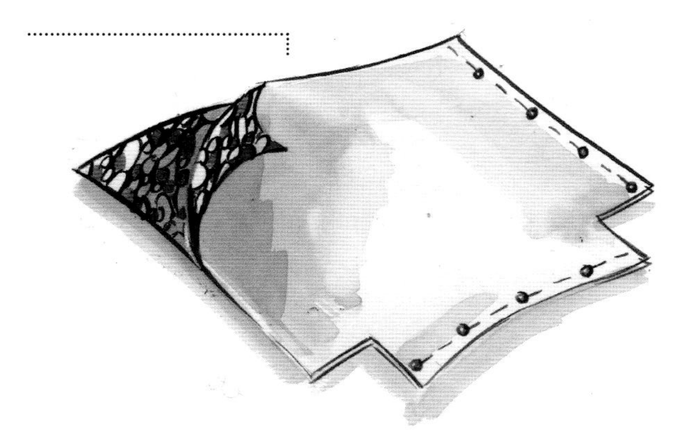

Stitching the bag pieces together Machine stitch these three long edges with a 1.5cm seam allowance, working a few reverse stitches at the ends of the seams. Then press the seams open.

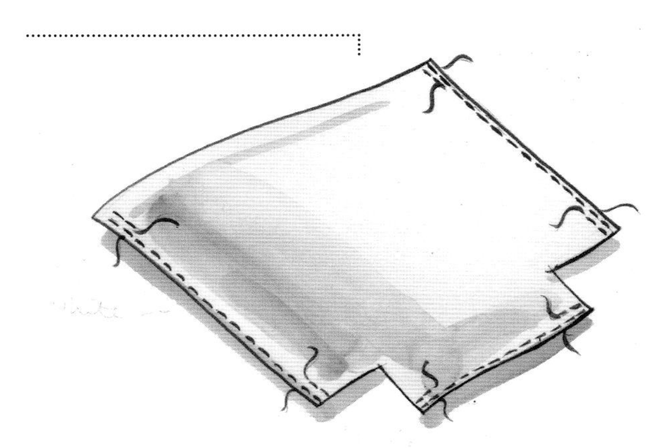

Stitching the t-junction seams at the bag base Open out the bag and refold one of the bag-base corners so that the ends of the side and bottom seams line up. Pin the two together with the seam allowances aligned and machine stitch, 1.5cm from the edge. Stitch the other corner in the same way.

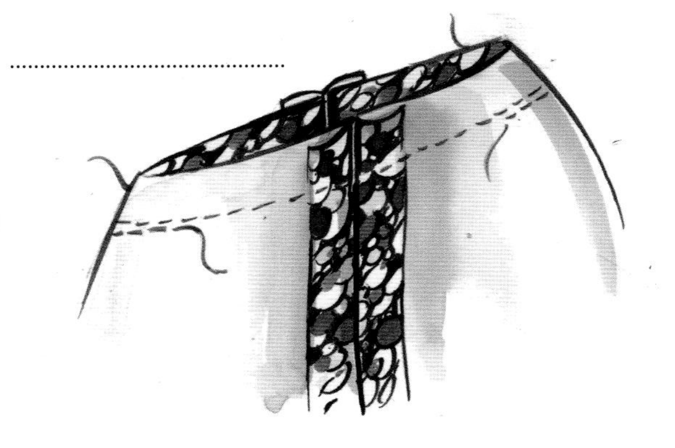

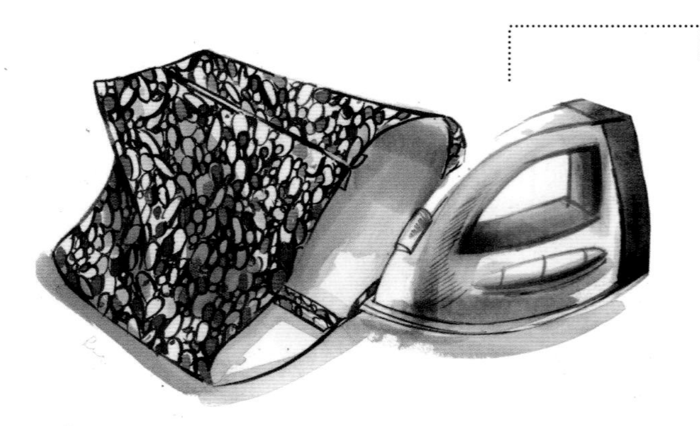

Hemming the top edge of the bag Turn the bag right side out. Fold over and press a 3cm turning around the top edge, then machine stitch it in place 3mm from the fold.

Attaching the handles Using double-sided tape, stick the ends of the handles to the top edge of the bag, following the guide marks on the pattern. Sew in place with matching quilting thread, working four or five backstitches through each pair of holes for strength. (Remove the double-sided tape before completing the stitching.)

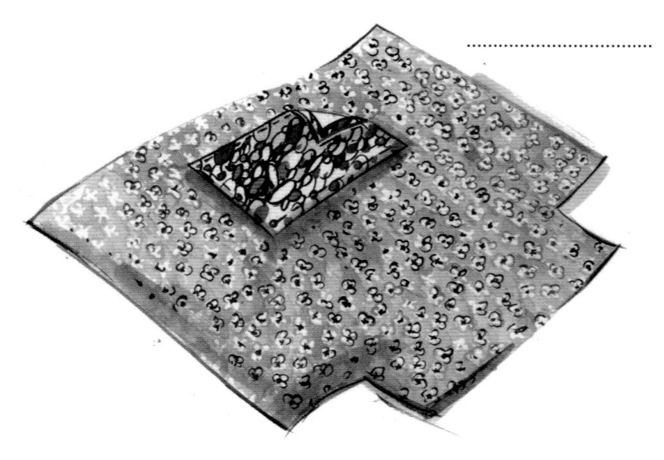

Making the lining Press under a 1cm turning along the side and bottom edges of the pocket piece. Then press a double 1cm hem along the top edge and machine stitch this in place. Pin the pocket centrally to the right side of one of the lining pieces, 9cm from the top edge. Machine stitch the pocket to the lining along the sides and bottom, 3mm from the fold. If you wish, divide the pocket with a central line of stitches to make a phone pocket. Stitch together the two lining pieces exactly as for the bag. Press back a 4cm turning round the top of the lining.

Taking it further

This tote has a secret – it is really two bags in one! You need two 28mm metal handbag press studs. Sew one half of each pair to the top front edge, 2cm from the top edge and 6cm from the side seams, and the other half to the top back edge in the corresponding positions. On the days when you don't need to carry much with you, simply fold in the corners and press the studs together to reduce the size.

Adding the lining If you wish, place a piece of stiff cardboard, 18 x 35cm, in the base of the bag before inserting the lining. The slip the lining inside bag, matching the side seams. Pin top edges together, so the lining sits just 1cm from the top edge of the bag. Slipstitch the lining to the bag.

● THE READY-MADE LEATHER HANDLES LEND A PROFESSIONAL FINISHING TOUCH TO THE BAG, BUT YOU COULD EASILY STITCH YOUR OWN FROM TWO 50 X 15CM STRIPS OF CONTRASTING OR MATCHING BAG FABRIC. MAKE THEM IN THE SAME WAY AS THE BEANBAG HANDLES ON PAGE 50, AND STITCH THEM TO THE BAG WITH REINFORCING STITCHING AT EACH END.

Organisation

Keepsake Board

This is not strictly a sewing project – in fact, there is no actual stitching involved – but this green baize noticeboard makes a great showcase for 'Elysian', a classic Liberty Tana Lawn that first appeared almost a century ago. It can be constructed to any size and would work equally well in an office, kitchen, busy hallway or child's bedroom.

Finished size

Approximately 40 x 60cm or preferred size

You will need

- For board covering, green baize (or felt) or other solid-coloured fabric (see Measuring Up and Cutting Out for fabric amount)
- For 'ribbon' strips, 25cm of Liberty Tana Lawn in 'Elysian', a lightweight cotton fabric in a small-scale print
- Wadding
- Cork pinboard, or rectangle of soft board, approximately 40 x 60cm or preferred size
- Staple gun
- Hammer and 17 decorative upholstery nails

Measuring up and cutting out

FROM WADDING:

- Cut 1 rectangle 3cm larger all around than board

FROM BOARD-COVERING FABRIC:

- Cut 1 rectangle 5cm larger all around than board

FROM TANA LAWN:

- Tear (or cut) fabric from selvedge-to-selvedge into five 5cm strips

NACRE
D'ORIENT

Covering the board with wadding Lay the wadding out flat and position the board centrally over it, facing downwards. Fold back the overlap along each edge and staple it to the back of the board, pulling it gently so that it lies taut. Mitre each corner as you reach it, by folding the fabric over at a 45-degree angle.

Covering the board with fabric Staple the board-covering fabric over the wadding in the same way. The edges of the fabric will overlap the wadding.

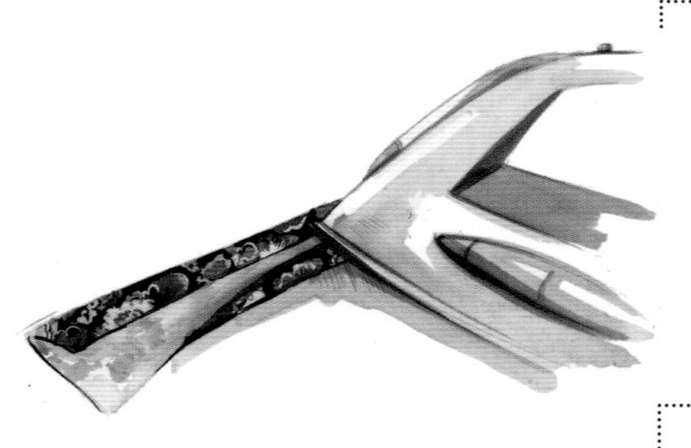

Preparing the 'ribbon' fabric strips Trim any stray threads from the 'ribbon' fabric strips and press them flat. Then press a 1.5cm turning along both long edges of each strip.

Stapling the fabric in place Cut a pressed strip of fabric to fit diagonally across the board, from corner to corner, allowing 10cm extra (5cm extra at each end) for the overlap. Place the strip in position on the board and staple the ends to the back of the board. The distance between the strips will depend on the size of the board you are using, but the best way to make a symmetrical diamond grid is to add two more evenly spaced parallel strips on each side of this diagonal. Use a quilter's ruler or a large draughtsman's triangle to measure the distance between them and mark the position with dressmaker's pins.

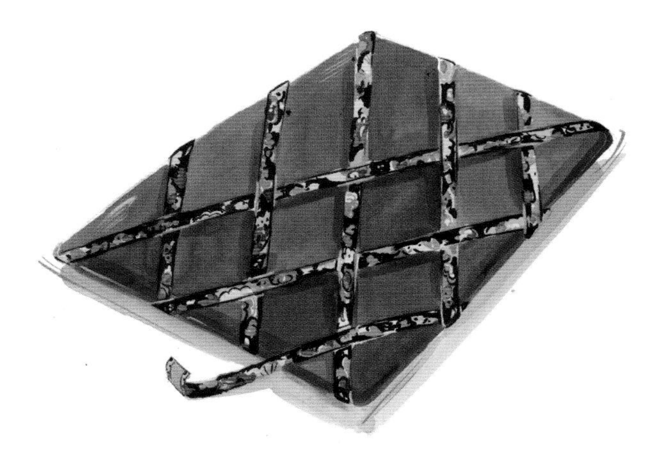

Taking it further

For a lighter overall look, cover your padded board with a length of Tana Lawn: large-scale floral designs, like 'Princess Emerald' or 'Kate Ada', are ideal. Pick out an interesting background or spot colour and choose a co-ordinating cotton tape or satin ribbon to weave the grid.

Completing the grid Complete the grid by adding five more interwoven strips in the opposite direction. Start at the centre as before, and take the longest strip under and over the others before stapling it down. Mark the position of the shorter strips, then weave them through and fix them down in the same way.

Finishing the board Add a little extra embellishment by hammering in a decorative upholstery nail at each intersection.

● TO HANG YOUR BOARD ON A WALL, SECURE IT IN PLACE WITH METAL PICTURE PLATES SO THAT IT LIES FLAT. IF YOU WANT TO DISPLAY IT AS HERE, PROPPED AGAINST A SHELF OR ON TOP OF A FIREPLACE, BE SURE TO FIX A COUPLE OF SCREWS OR A STRIP OF WOOD IN FRONT OF IT, SO THAT IT WON'T SLIP FORWARD AND FALL OFF.

Jewellery Roll

Keep the highlights of your jewellery collection safely together when you are travelling, by storing them in this practical padded roll. It has a zip-up compartment for necklaces, a secure ring holder and three pockets for brooches or earrings. This is one of those useful projects that you might intend making for a friend but end up keeping for yourself!

Finished size

20 x 32cm, when opened out

You will need

- For main fabric, 23 x 70cm Liberty Tana Lawn in 'Eleanabella', a lightweight cotton fabric in a medium-scale print
- For lining, 23 x 60cm in a solid-coloured lightweight cotton fabric
- For binding, 15 x 90cm contrasting solid-coloured lightweight silk for binding
- Quilt wadding, 25 x 40cm
- Matching sewing threads
- 20cm zip
- Small amount of polyester toy filling
- One 9mm press stud
- Two or three 9mm glass beads with large holes

Cutting out

FROM MAIN FABRIC:

- Cut 1 outer panel, 22 x 34cm
- Cut 1 inner-lining panel, 20 x 32cm
- Cut 1 pocket panel binding, 3 x 20cm

FROM WADDING:

- Cut 1 piece, 20 x 32cm

FROM LINING FABRIC:

- Cut 1 short lining-panel, 20 x 12cm
- Cut 1 long lining-panel, 20 x 22cm
- Cut 1 pocket, 20 x 11cm
- Cut 1 ring holder strip, 6 x 20cm

FROM BINDING FABRIC:

- Cut 2 strips, each 3 x 34cm, for binding long edges

Cut 2 strips, each 3 x 22cm, for binding short edges
Cut 1 strip, 3.5 x 88cm, for ties

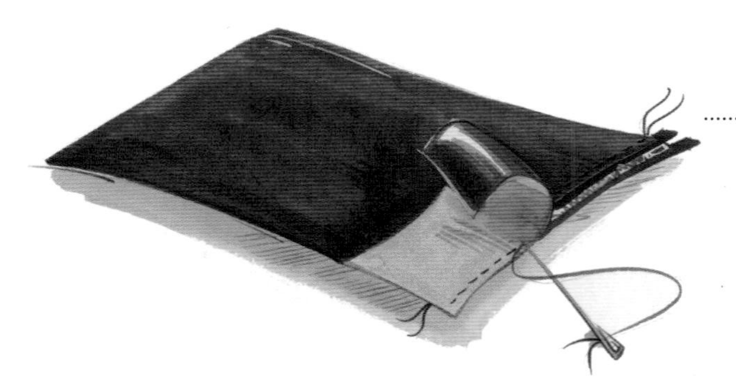

Stitching the zip to the lining Following the method used for the washbag on page 42, tack, then machine stitch the two inside panels to the zip, with the large panel on the left and the small on the right, and using a 1cm seam allowance along the zip. Topstitch with matching sewing thread and press lightly.

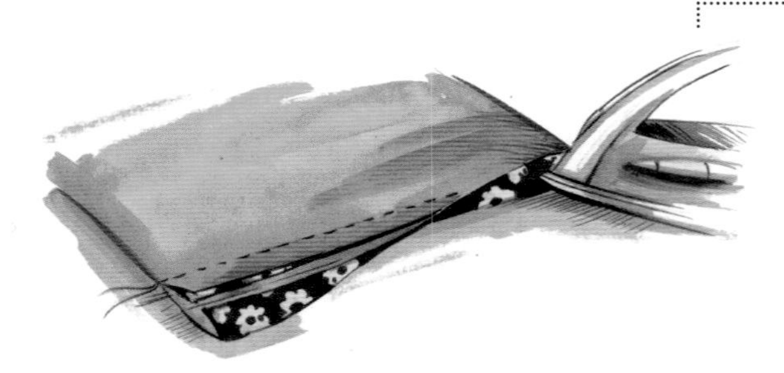

Binding the lining pocket Press the floral binding strip for the lining pocket panel in half lengthways with the wrong side on the inside. Unfold and press one long edge inwards so that it meets the centre fold. With right sides together, pin the raw edge of the binding (the edge without the folded back seam allowance) to one edge of the pocket and stitch them together with a 6mm seam. Turn the folded-hem edge of the binding over to the wrong side of the pocket so that it encloses the raw edges and re-press the fold. Tack down and slipstitch the folded edge in place. Remove the tacking.

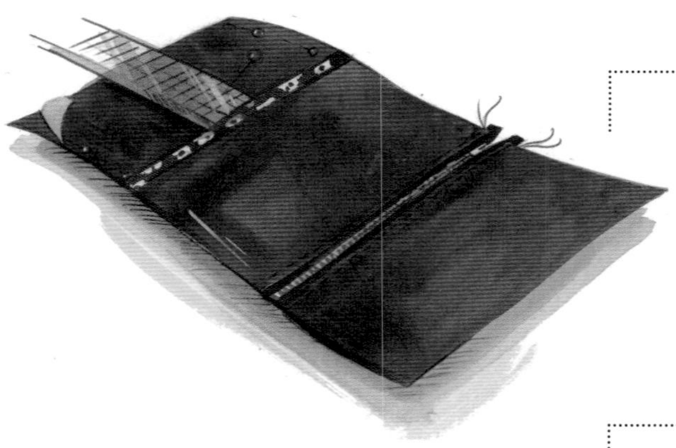

Stitching the compartment divisions on the pockets Pin the wrong side of the pocket to the right side of the end of the long lining panel, with the binding facing inwards. Mark two stitch lines across the pocket, each 7cm from the long edges of the lining. Do this with a dressmaker's pen or by scoring a line against the ruler with a pin. Machine stitch along the two marked lines to create three compartments in the pocket.

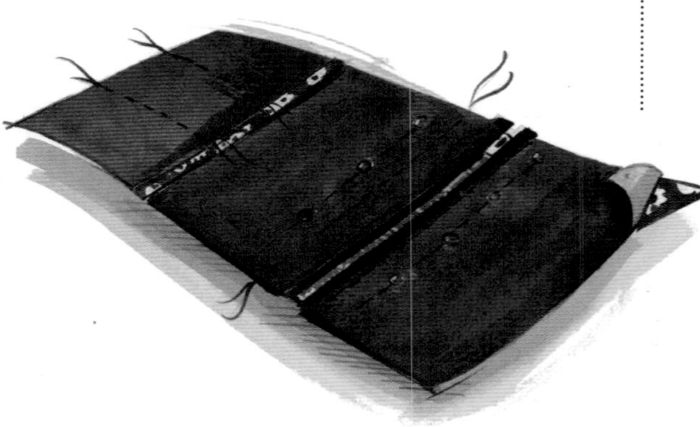

Adding the main fabric inner-lining panel Lay the main fabric inner-lining panel right side up and place the finished lining right side up on top of it; trim the lining on top to the same size as the main fabric piece, taking any excess length from the pocket end. Pin the two together on each side of the zip and machine stitch 1.5cm from the inner edge of the zip. This creates the separate zipped pocket.

● IF YOU INTEND TO TRAVEL WITH A LOT OF BLING, YOU CAN EXTEND THE LENGTH OF THE FABRIC AND MAKE AN EXTRA ROW OF POCKETS OR AN ENLARGED ZIP-UP COMPARTMENT.

Making the ring holder With right sides together, pin the two long edges of the ring holder strip together and machine stitch with a 6mm seam allowance. Fold one end so that the seam is central, then machine stitch across the end of the tube 6mm from the edge as shown. Turn the tube right side out and stuff with polyester filling. With the seam at centre back, machine stitch across the opening 5mm from the edge.

Stitching the ring holder to the lining Pin the raw edge of the ring holder to the lining about 2cm from the top of the zip. Stitch securely in place, about 5mm from the edge. Sew the bottom part of the press stud to the lining, and the top part to the back of the ring holder, ensuring that they are in line with each other.

Assembling the layers Place the main fabric outer panel face down on the work surface with the wadding centred on top of it. Position the prepared lining face up on top. Pin and tack all the layers together around the outer edge. Trim the layers to the same size as the lining.

Binding the outer edge and adding the ties Trim the two longest binding strips to the same length as the long edges of the jewellery roll and stitch them on as you did for the pocket binding. Bind the short edges in the same way, but fold under the extra 1cm at each end of the binding and sew these folded edges together when complete. To make the ties, fold the tie strip in half widthways with the right sides facing inwards and machine stitch the long edges together with a 1cm seam. Trim the seam allowance back to 5mm and turn the fabric tube right side out with a safety pin, tapestry needle and thread or a rouleaux maker. Press, so that the seams lie along one edge. Fold the tie in half and stitch securely to the centre of the short edge closest to the zip. (If desired, thread a single bead onto both ties at once and slide it down to the edge of the jewellery roll.) Slide a bead onto the end of each individual tie, knot the ends securely, slide the beads close to the knots and trim the tie ends at a sharp angle.

Drawstring Bag

Whether you are sorting out the children's toy cupboard, tidying up the laundry or packing a suitcase for the summer holidays, you're bound to find a good use for a drawstring bag of one size or another. They are indispensable for storing away all kinds of household items and look far more attractive than a lot of plastic shopping bags. Needlecord, with its fine velvety pile and slightly stretchy weave, is an ideal fabric for these bags, and the satin ribbon ties look prettier than an ordinary cotton tape or ready-made cord.

Finished size

- 23cm wide by 39.5cm long, including the bag's top border

You will need

- 55 x 40cm piece of Liberty Rossmore Cord in 'Penny', a lightweight fine-ribbed corduroy, in a mini print
- 55 x 20cm piece of Liberty Rossmore Cord in a contrasting shade of 'Penny'
- Matching sewing thread
- 110cm of 1.5cm wide double-faced satin ribbon
- Large tapestry needle or safety pin

Cutting out

FROM MAIN FABRIC:

- Cut 1 main bag piece 48 x 34cm

FROM CONTRASTING FABRIC:

- Cut 1 bag top 48 x 17cm

NOTE: Seam allowance (1cm) is included in the cutting size.

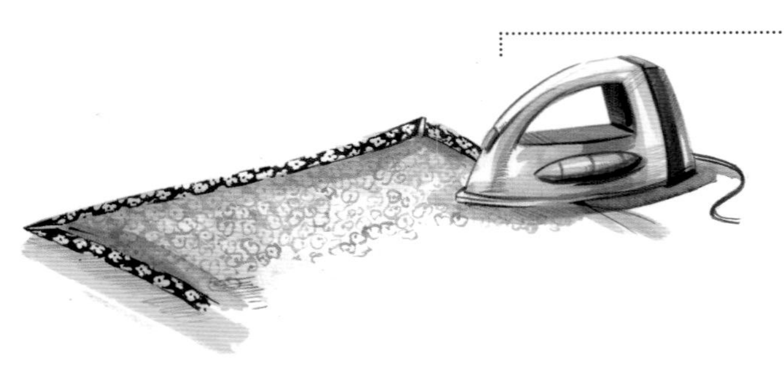

Preparing the bag top Press under a 1cm turning along the short side edges and one long edge of the bag top piece, mitring the corners as shown on page 151 of the techniques section.

Joining the bag top to the main bag piece Unfold the pressed-under seam allowance on the short ends of the bag top and pin the unpressed long edge of the bag top to the top edge of the main bag piece, with right sides together. Machine stitch, leaving a 1cm seam allowance. Then press the seam upwards.

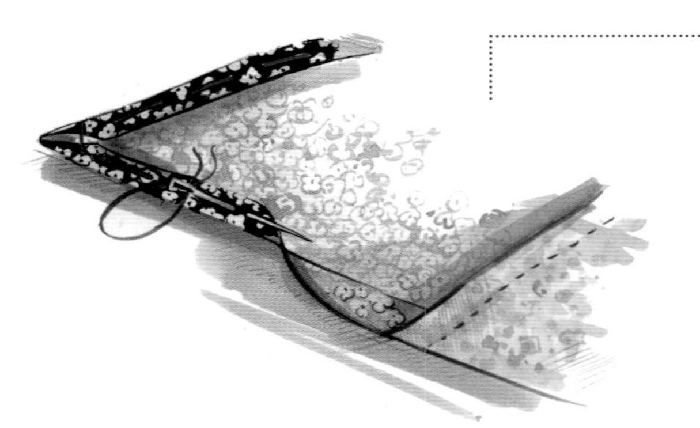

Tacking the bag top seam allowances in place Refold the creases around the side and top edges of the bag top and tack them down.

Tacking the bag top to the main bag piece Fold the bag top over to the wrong side of the main bag piece, so that the folded top edge lies about 6mm below the seam and press. Then pin and tack the long tacked edge of the bag top to the main bag piece.

Stitching the drawstring channel Working from the right side of the bag, machine stitch along the seam between the bag top and the main piece (to hide the stitching) – this forms the bottom stitching line of the channel. Mark the top stitching line of the channel 2cm above this, using a chalk pencil. Starting at the right top corner and machine stitching 3mm from the edge, sew the front and back of the bag top together as far as the marked line, turn at a right angle and stitch along the line, then back up to the left corner.

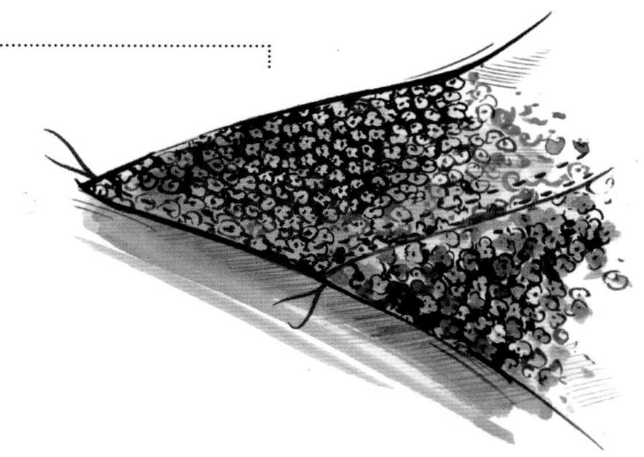

Finishing the drawstring bag Fold the bag in half widthways with right sides together and pin the side and bottom edges together. Machine stitch with a 1cm seam allowance, ending the seam as close to the bag top as possible. Press back the unstitched seam allowance at the top of the main bag piece and machine stitch around it 3mm from the folded edge. Remove the tacking. Turn the bag right side out and press lightly.

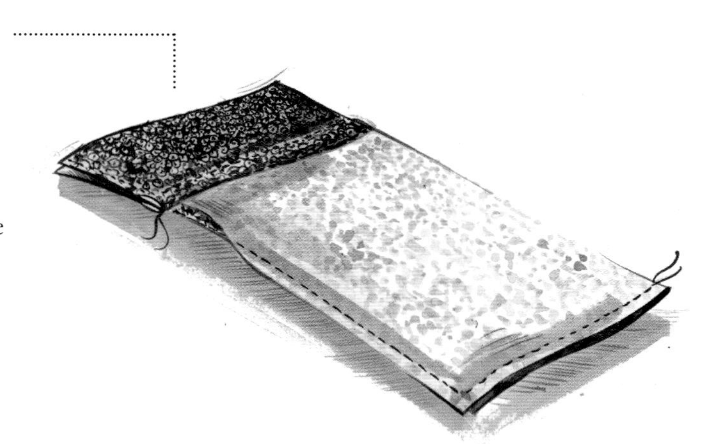

Inserting the ribbon Thread the ribbon through a large tapestry needle (or fasten a safety pin to one end of the ribbon). Push the needle (or safety pin) all the way around the drawstring channel. Then tie the two ends of the ribbon together in a bow. Trim each end of the ribbon at a diagonal to the preferred length.

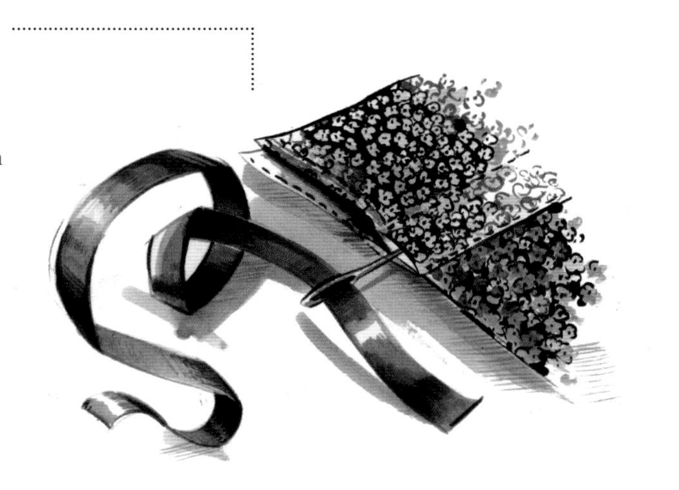

• KEEP YOUR HOUSEHOLD IN ORDER BY MAKING DRAWSTRING BAGS FOR EVERY MEMBER OF THE FAMILY, WITH AN EMBROIDERED NAME OR CONTENTS LABEL SEWN TO EACH ONE. THESE CAN BE HUNG ON A PEG RAIL IN THE HALLWAY OR KITCHEN, SO THERE WILL BE NO EXCUSES FOR LOST SHOES OR GAMES KIT.

Gadget Case

You'll find many different types of protective case for mobile phones, tablet computers and other gadgets on the market, but making your own padded cover is a simple process and gives an everyday object just that little more style and individual flair. Follow the steps below to make a sleeve for a music player or laptop: the method is the same for any size of gadget.

Finished size

Adjustable to fit any size mobile phone or small gadget

You will need

- For main fabric for outer case, leather, faux leather or printed canvas (see Measuring Up and Cutting Out for fabric amount)
- For lining, Liberty Tana Lawn in 'Wiltshire', a lightweight cotton fabric in a small-scale print
- For binding, Liberty Tana Lawn in 'Capel' or 'Wiltshire', a small-scale print
- Quilt wadding for padding
- Dressmaker's pattern paper
- Matching sewing thread
- Fabric glue stick

Cutting out

FROM OUTER CASE FABRIC:

- Cut 2 rectangles using the outer case pattern piece (see overleaf)

FROM WADDING:

- Cut 2 rectangles, using the outer case pattern piece (see overleaf)

FROM LINING FABRIC:

- Cut 2 rectangles, using the lining pattern piece (see overleaf)

FROM BINDING:

- Cut 1 strip 4cm wide to required binding length

Measuring up

PATTERN PIECE OF OUTER CASE

Place your gadget on the dressmaker's pattern paper so that it is lined up with the printed grid. Draw around the outside edge of the gadget, allowing a little extra all around for half the thickness of the item. Remove the gadget and square off the corners on the outline. Then add a second outline 1cm outside the first for the seam allowance (the top edge has no seam allowance but this allows the gadget to sit 1cm inside the case). Cut out this pattern piece for the outer case.

PATTERN PIECE OF LINING

Lay the outer case pattern piece on dressmaker's paper and draw around it. Then add an extra 4cm along the top edge to make the turnback (for a small gadget you could add only 3cm extra for the top turnback if preferred). Cut out this pattern piece for the lining.

BINDING LENGTH

Measure around the two side and the bottom edges of the outer case pattern piece; this is the length of the binding strip.

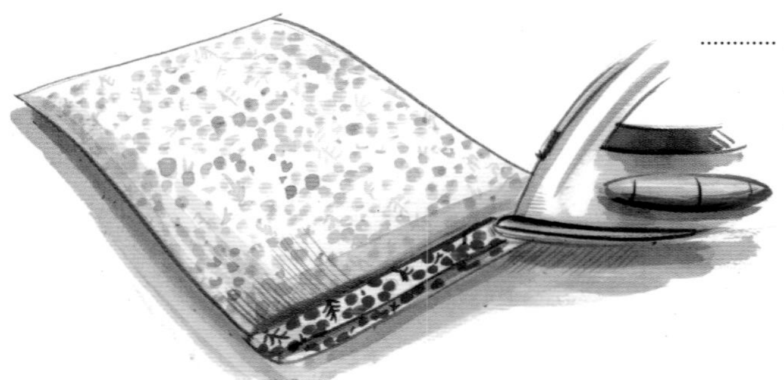

Making the lining With right sides together, pin the two lining pieces together around the side and bottom edges. Machine stitch, leaving a 6mm seam allowance. Press under a 1cm turning around the opening.

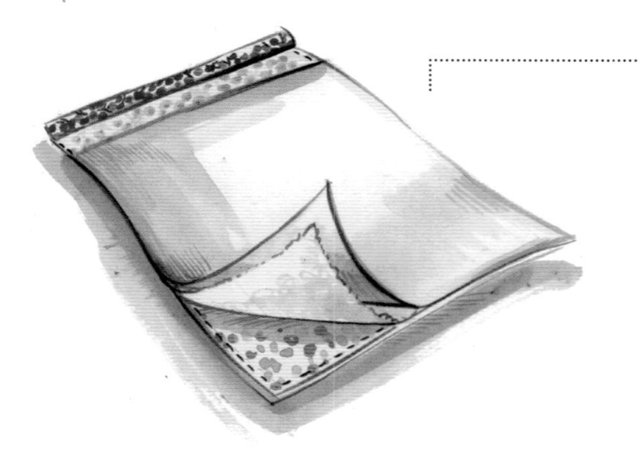

Assembling the layers Now sandwich together all the five layers. Start by placing an outside piece, face downwards, on your table. Position a rectangle of wadding exactly on top of this, then add the stitched lining, matching up the side and bottom edges. The second layer of wadding goes on next, then the second outside piece, face upwards.

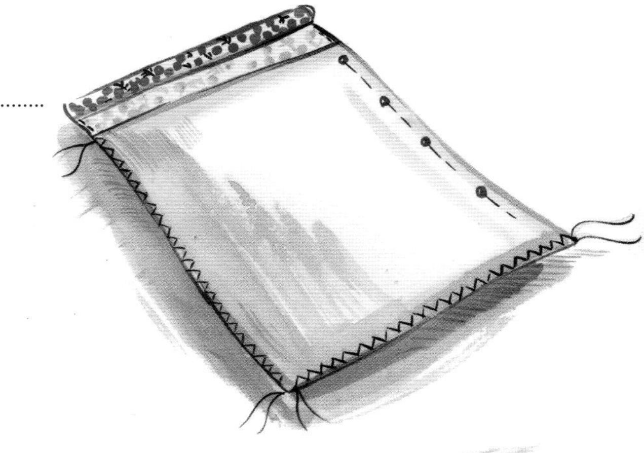

Stitching the bag layers together Pin the layers together along the sides and bottom. Set your machine to a wide zigzag and if your outer case is leather, fit a leather needle on your sewing machine (this is useful, but not essential). Stitch slowly and carefully along the bottom edge, removing one pin at a time as you proceed. Sew the side edges from the corners to the top of the outer case to prevent any puckering at the bottom edge.

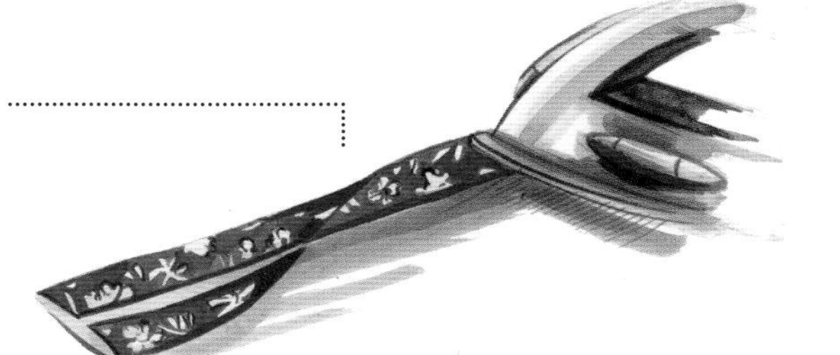

Preparing the fabric binding Press the binding strip in half lengthways with the right sides together and unfold. Press the raw edges inwards so that they line up with the centre crease, then press the binding in half again.

Binding the edges Fixing the fabric around the edges of the bag is a fiddly process, so it's time for a bit of cheating. Run a fabric glue stick lightly along the inside, turned back, edges of the binding, so that they will adhere to the bag without pins or tacking. Starting at one top corner, wrap it around the zigzagged edges of the bag. Mitre the corners neatly, using a little more glue to keep the angles sharp. Machine stitch down, 3mm from the inside edge, using a matching sewing thread.

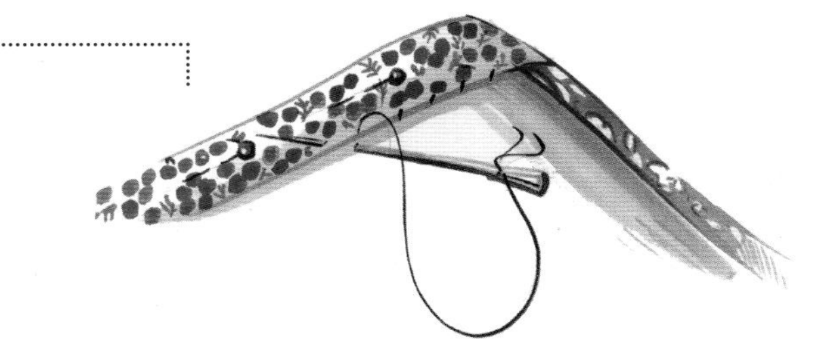

Finishing off the opening Trim the ends of the binding so that they are in line with the top of the bag, then fold the turnback to the right side of the case. Pin it down, making sure that the depth is the same all the way around. Hand sew the folded edge to the bag with tiny, unobtrusive stitches.

Peacock Pincushion

The peacock, with its iridescent blue feathers and flamboyant tail, is an iconic symbol of the Aesthetic Movement, which appears widely in paintings, jewellery and textile designs of the late nineteenth century. This quirky pincushion may lack the sinuous grace of his Victorian predecessors, but I'm sure that he will prove a useful sewing companion. The 'eyes' on his sequinned tail are cut from Liberty's 'Caesar' Tana Lawn, the contemporary reworking of 'Hera', Arthur Silver's 1887 peacock feather furnishing print.

You will need

- For peacock's body, 23 x 80cm piece of Liberty Tana Lawn in 'Pepper', a lightweight cotton fabric in a mini print
- For feathers, 15 x 85cm piece of solid-coloured heavy-weight (furnishing-weight) fabric
- For feather appliqué, 25 x 40cm piece of Liberty Tana Lawn in 'Caesar' (piece cut to include three sizes of feather), a medium-scale peacock-feather print with different feather sizes in print
- Scraps of white and turquoise felt, for eyes
- Matching sewing threads
- Turquoise and navy sewing threads, for embroidery
- Polyester toy filling
- Florist's wire and wire cutters
- Pearl and glass-headed pins
- Translucent sequins in different sizes and shapes

Making pattern pieces

Trace and cut out paper templates for the body, base gusset, three feathers, three feather appliqué pieces, eye and inner eye. Transfer all the markings and letters.

Cutting out

FROM PRINT FOR PEACOCK'S BODY:

- Cut 2 rectangles, each 23 x 25cm
- Cut 1 base gusset

FROM HEAVY-WEIGHT FEATHER FABRIC:

- Cut 7 large feathers
- Cut 6 medium-size feathers
- Cut 4 small feathers

FROM APPLIQUÉ PRINT:

When cutting appliqué pieces, centre the template shape on the large, medium-size or small feather motifs in the fabric print.

- Cut 7 large feather appliqué pieces
- Cut 6 medium-size appliqué feather pieces
- Cut 4 small feather appliqué pieces

FROM WHITE FELT:

- Cut 2 eyes

FROM TURQUOISE FELT:

- Cut 2 inner eyes

NOTE: THE TEMPLATES ARE SHOWN HERE AT 50%; ENLARGE TO 200% ON A PHOTOCOPIER TO ACHIEVE CORRECT SIZE.

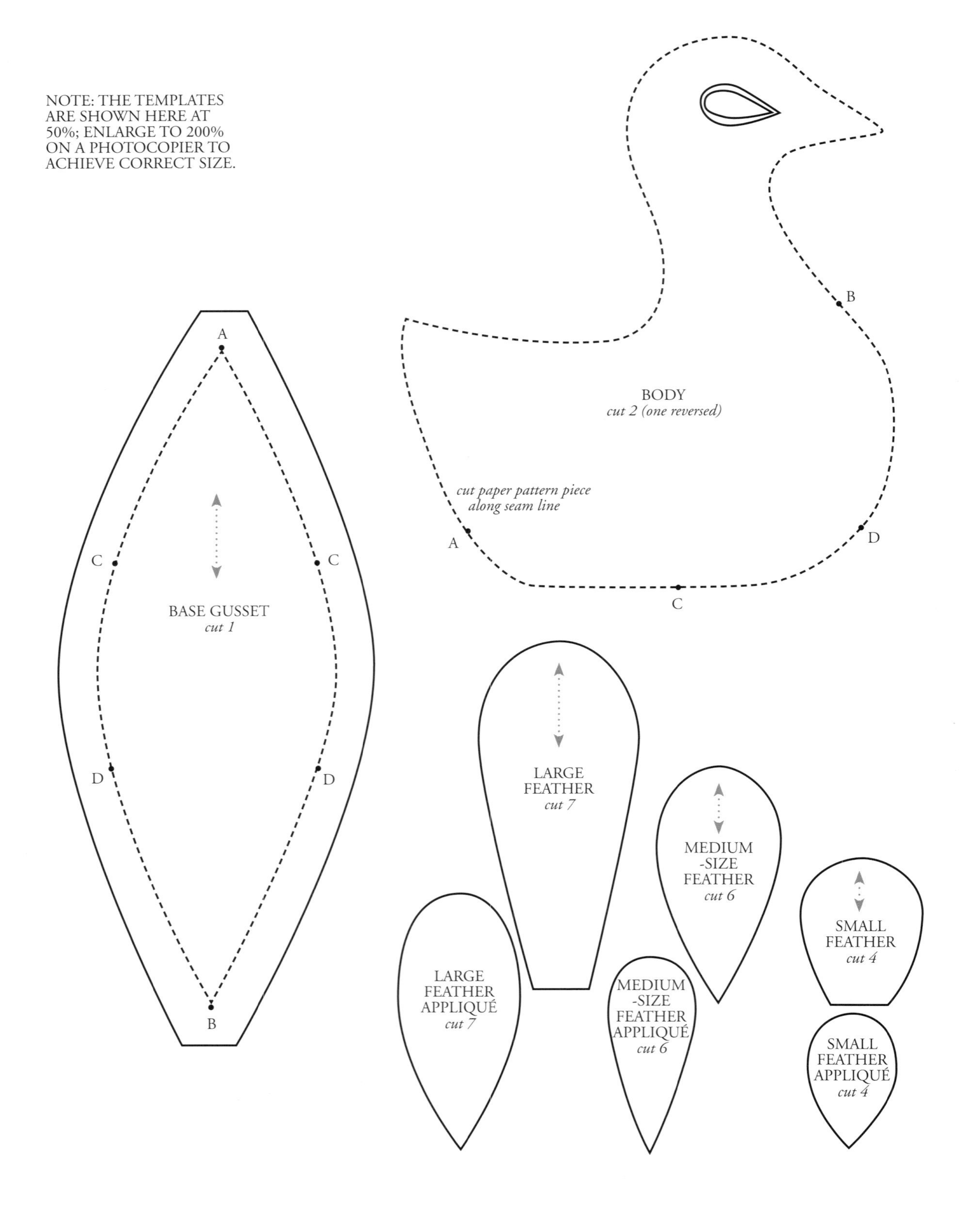

Stitching and cutting out the body Place the two pieces of body fabric together, with right sides together and edges aligned. Pin on the body pattern piece, making sure there is a 1cm margin between the pins and the edge of the template. Working a few reverse stitches at each end of the seam, machine stitch around the back, head and neck between points A and B, as close as possible to the paper. Cut the body out, leaving a 1.5cm seam allowance all around the edge of the paper. Cut tiny notches in the seam allowances in line with C and D on the body piece, then remove the pattern piece.

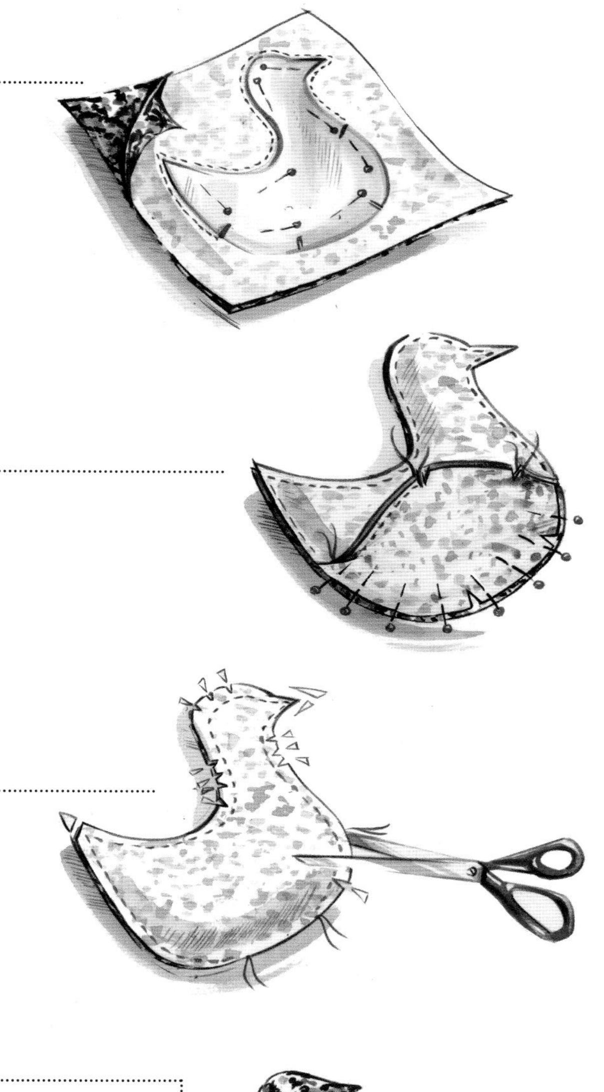

Adding the gusset Pin one side of the base gusset to the body, with right sides together, matching up the tips of the gusset with points A and B, and matching up the C and D notches. Tack in place from A to C and B to D, leaving C to D open. (The opening between C and D will be used to stuff the body.) Machine stitch 1.5cm from the edge. Stitch the other side of the gusset in place, but pin, tack and stitch along the entire seam line, from A to B.

Trimming the seam allowance Trim the seam allowance to 1cm. To give the curved seams a smooth finish, snip small triangles into the sharpest curves around the head, neck and chest and clip the surplus fabric from the beak and tail, but don't cut any closer than 3mm or the seams may split. Remove the tacking. Press under the seam allowance along both sides of the opening, then turn the body right side out.

Stuffing the bird Stuff the body firmly with polyester toy filling. Use just a little at a time, so that the bird doesn't become lumpy and use the eraser end of a pencil to push the fibres right into the head, neck and tail. When the bird is nice and plump, tack the two edges of the opening together, slipstitch closed and remove the tacking.

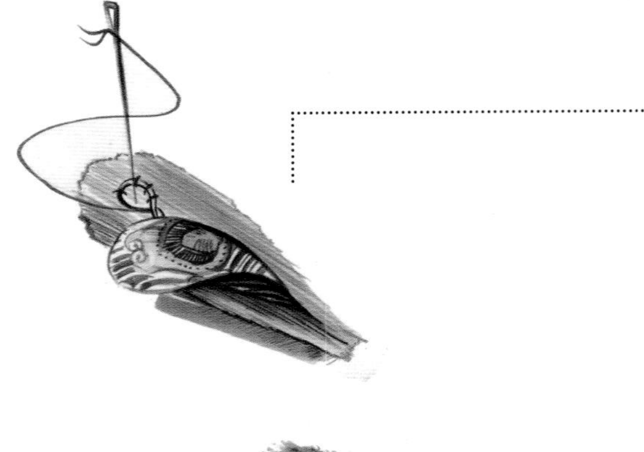

Preparing the feathers The seven large and six medium-size feathers are all reinforced with wire so that they will stand out proudly. For each one, cut a piece of florist's wire roughly the same length as the feather appliqué shape. Twist the top into a small loop and stitch the wire to the feather, 2cm down from the top edge. Checking that the bottom of the wire doesn't protrude, roughly tack the feather appliqué piece over the wire. Tack a feather appliqué piece to each of the four small feathers as well, omitting the wire.

Embroidering the feathers You could simply stitch around the edge of the feather appliqué to secure it in place, but a little simple machine embroidery gives texture and an extra dimension to the tail. Using navy and then turquoise thread, stitch extra fronds either side of the feather spine and around the 'eye' (taking care to avoid the wire). If you prefer to embroider by hand, work random straight stitches in the same direction as the printed fronds.

Sewing on the tail Sew the base of the first large feather to the body, 2cm down from the tip of the body. Then overlapping the feathers slightly, sew three more large feathers in place on each side, to create a fanned tail. Use long stab stitches and sew from front to back to make the tail really secure. Add the six medium-size feathers so that the 'eyes' lie between the large feathers, then add three small ones in between the medium-size feathers. The final small feather goes in the centre.

Adding the finishing touches Sew one white felt eye to each side of the head with small hand stitches, then sew on the inner eyes. Insert a pearl-topped pin in each eye to represent the shiny pupils. Finish off by sewing a sprinkling of translucent sequins across the tail feathers and adding a crest of pearl-topped pins. Stick the rest of the pins into the peacock's breast to complete his fine plumage.

Book Covers

A desk piled high with stacks of files, standard stationery, diaries and ruled notebooks is not very conducive to work, particularly if your office is at home. Transforming your books with patterned fabric may not make your mundane tasks any quicker, but it is guaranteed to cheer up the daily routine. You can then go on to make covers to protect your favourite hardback novel, a much-loved volume of poetry and a precious childhood story, and fill a whole shelf with Liberty prints.

Finished size

Adjustable to fit any size book

You will need

- Liberty Tana Lawn in 'Helena's Party', 'Mitsi' or 'Willow's Garden', a lightweight cotton fabric in a print (see Measuring Up for fabric amount)
- Matching sewing thread

Measuring up

SLIP COVER PIECE

- width = height of book, plus 4cm for hems
- length = four times width of front cover, plus width of spine

Cutting out

Cut 1 rectangular slip cover piece for each book cover.

- GIVE A TATTERED (BUT NOT VALUABLE!) BOOK A LUXURIOUSLY PADDED FEEL BY CUTTING A RECTANGLE OF QUILT WADDING OR THICK WOVEN FABRIC TO FIT AROUND THE FRONT, BACK AND SPINE. GLUE THIS IN PLACE BEFORE MAKING THE SLIP COVER.

LIBERTY

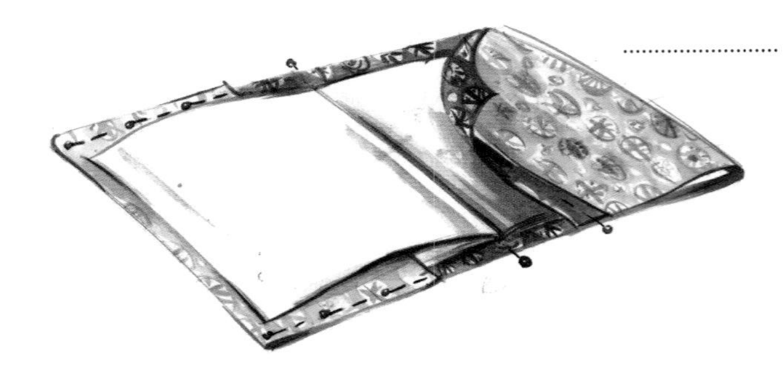

Marking the fabric centre Fold the fabric in half widthways and mark the centre of the long edges with pins. Press a 3cm turning to the wrong side along each short edge.

Pinning the cover With the right side facing the book, wrap the fabric around the back and front covers of the book, lining the pins up with the centre of the spine. Pin the front and back of the fabric together along the top and bottom edges of the cover.

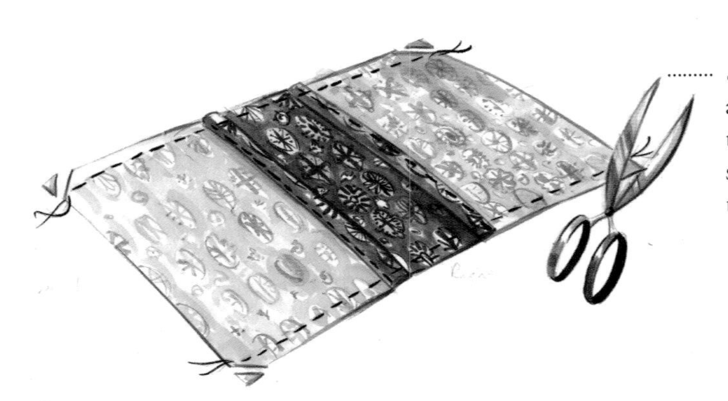

Stitching the cover Slide the cover off the book and tack along the four pinned lines. Machine stitch right across the top and bottom of the cover, working a few reverse stitches at each end of each seam. Then clip a small triangle from each corner. Remove the tacking.

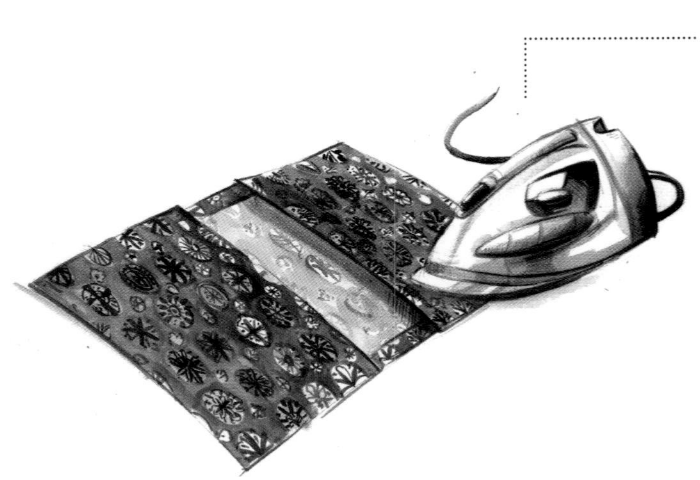

Pressing the cover Turn the cover right side out and ease out the corners into neat right angles. Press the seams and press back the top and bottom hems at the spine along the machine stitches.

Slipping the cover on Fold back the front and back covers of your book and slip the fabric cover in place.

Luxury

Round Cushion

This sumptuous circular cushion is surprisingly easy to sew and would make an impressive-looking project for a novice. It is made from twelve narrow strips of Liberty Tana Lawn and filled with a soft round feather pad. And there's not a curved seam in sight! The three fabrics – one light, one mid-tone and one dark – have very different designs but they share a similar colour palette, so work harmoniously together.

Finished size

45cm in diameter by 5cm deep

You will need

- 30cm of Liberty Tana Lawn in 'Rueben', 'David Joe' and 'Mitsi', a lightweight cotton fabric, in each of three small-scale prints
- Matching sewing thread
- Cushion pad 45cm in diameter x 5cm deep
- Two 4–5cm buttons
- Buttonhole thread

Cutting out

- Cut 4 panels, each 14 x 54cm, from each of the three fabrics for a total of 12 panels.

NOTE: Seam allowance (1cm) is included in the cutting size.

- IF YOUR FABRIC HAS A DIRECTIONAL DESIGN AND YOU WANT THE LINES OR STRIPS TO RADIATE OUR FROM THE CENTRE OF YOUR CUSHION, BE SURE TO CUT OUT THE PANELS SO THAT THIS PATTERN RUNS LENGTHWAYS ALONG THE PANEL. YOU MAY HAVE TO ADJUST THE FABRIC AMOUNT TO ACCOMMODATE THIS.

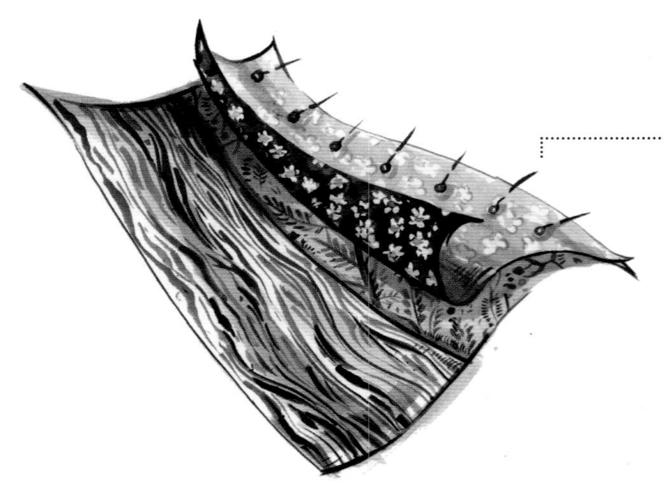

Joining the panels together Select three panels, one in each of the three different fabrics. With right sides together, pin two of these panels together along one long edge. Machine stitch, leaving a 1cm seam allowance. Stitch the third panel to the right edge of the second panel in the same way. Add on the remaining nine panels, repeating the same sequence of three fabrics to form a repeating pattern. Machine stitch the first and twelfth panels together to form a cylinder. Press all the seams open and keep the cylinder wrong side out.

Gathering one end of the cover Thread a needle with a 1m length of sewing thread. Sew a line of long running stitches around the cylinder, 1cm from one edge. Gather the fabric gently as you proceed. When you have sewn all around the edge, pull up the thread tightly. Stitch through the gathers several times to secure, then fasten off the thread.

Gathering the other end of the cover Turn the cover right side out. Place the cushion pad inside and adjust the position so that it lies perfectly central. Gather up the top edge as before. Push the raw edges through to the wrong side of the cover and finish off securely.

Adding the buttons Using a double length of buttonhole thread and a long crewel needle (with a large eye and sharp point), sew one of the buttons to the centre front so that it covers the gathering point. Carefully push the needle straight through to the back, so that it comes out at the centre of the gathers. You'll need to squeeze up the cushion pad to do this, and you may find a thimble helps you poke the needle right through. Sew on the other button and push the needle back to the front. Pull the thread so that the buttons sink right into the cushion, then wind it around the front button and fasten off.

Taking it further

You can give your cushion a bolder, more stripey look by using just two different fabrics: one light and one dark. Try this with two contrasting shades of 'Edenham'.

● THE MOTHER-OF-PEARL BUTTONS, WHICH ONCE FASTENED AN EDWARDIAN COAT, PROVIDE THE FOCAL POINT OF THE CUSHION. LOOK OUT FOR SIMILAR VINTAGE BUTTONS TO MATCH YOUR CHOSEN FABRICS, OR GO FOR A CONTEMPORARY ALTERNATIVE IN RESIN, WOOD OR METAL.

Rose Corsage

Halfway between fabric sculpture and embroidery, this three-dimensional flower is surprisingly straightforward to assemble and would make a dramatic accessory for either day or evening wear. The curled petals are cut from a double-sided layer of floral fabric – created by bonding together two different lightweight cotton prints with fusible adhesive web – and set into shape with a warm iron. Choose two non-directional prints with similar colour schemes, one with a tiny print and the other with a larger-scale design.

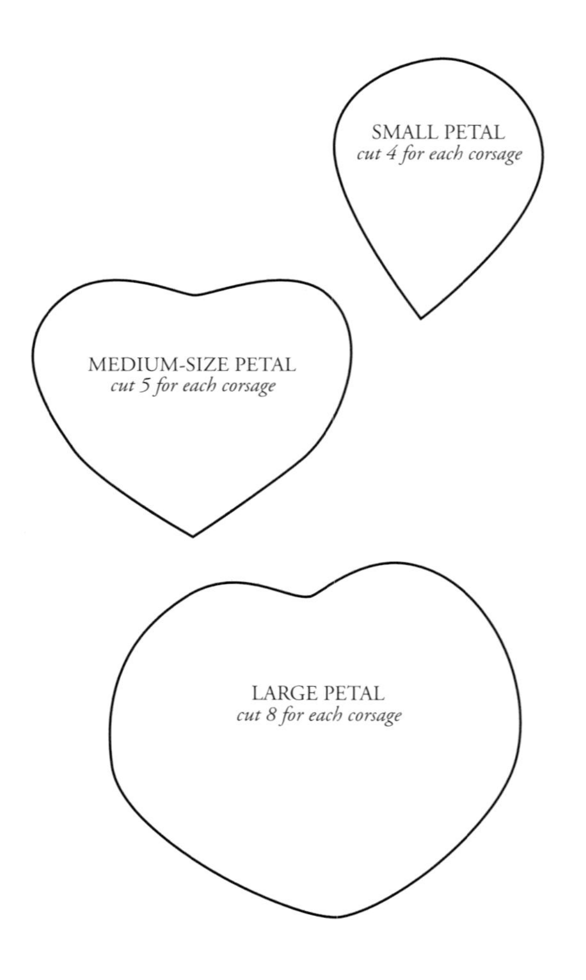

Finished size

Approximately 12.5cm in diameter

You will need

- 60 x 30cm piece of Liberty Tana Lawn in 'Penny', a lightweight cotton fabric, in a mini print
- 60 x 30cm piece of Liberty Tana Lawn in 'Toria', in a toning small-scale print
- 60 x 30cm piece of paper-backed fusible adhesive bonding web
- Matching sewing thread
- Tracing paper and pencil (optional)
- A medium-size knitting needle
- Brooch-back pin or small safety pin

Cutting out

Prepare the layered fabric, then trace and cut out the petals as explained on page 92.

- Cut 4 small petals
- Cut 5 medium-size petals
- Cut 8 large petals

NOTE: THE PETAL TEMPLATES ARE SHOWN HERE AT 50%; ENLARGE THEM ON A PHOTOCOPIER TO 200% TO ACHIEVE THE CORRECT SIZE.

Preparing the layered fabric The double-sided petals are made by fusing together the two different cotton prints. Following the manufacturer's instructions for the heat setting, iron the fusible adhesive bonding web onto the wrong side of the first fabric and peel off the paper: if it doesn't come off easily, iron it once more to soften the adhesive. Place the second fabric, right side upwards, on top of the wrong side of the first, and press it in place.

Cutting out the petals Photocopy or trace the full-size rose petal outlines and cut out three paper templates. Using these as a your guide, cut four small, five medium-size and eight large petals from the layered fabric.

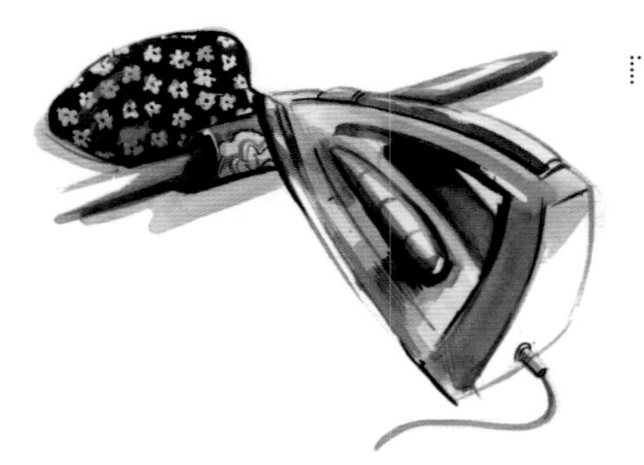

Shaping the small inner petals The two innermost small petals of the rose are tightly curled. With the right side of the layered fabric (the side you want showing on top of the rose) facing upwards starting at a long side edge of a small petal, wrap the petal lengthways tightly around the knitting needle. Press in the curve by running the tip of a hot iron over the fabric, as you slowly roll the needle all the way across the petal. Tightly curl a second small petal in the same way.

Shaping the outer petals The two remaining small petals and all the medium-size and large petals are all curled outwards around the top edge. To shape each petal, first place it right side face down, then roll the top right corner of the petal over the knitting needle, diagonally inwards a little (towards the petal base), and press. Curl the top left corner of each petal in the same way.

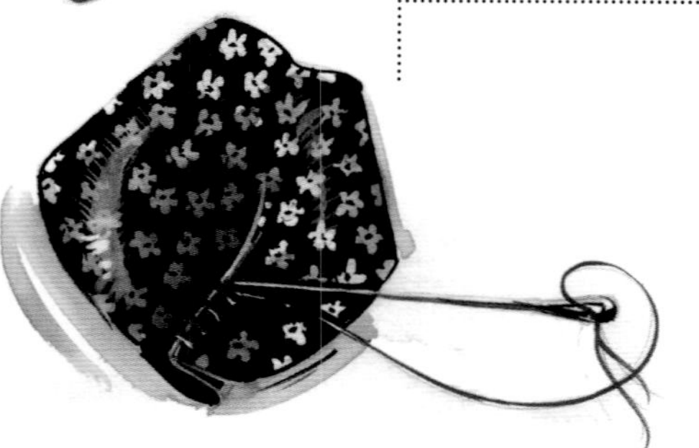

Pleating the petals Give extra depth to the five medium-size petals by folding down a small vertical pleat at the lower edge and stitching it in place with a matching sewing thread.

Assembling the bloom centre Start assembling the bloom with the two tightly curled small petals. Using matching sewing thread, stitch several times through the bottom end of the first rolled-up petal, 1cm from the base. Wrap the second tightly curled small petal loosely around the first and stitch securely in place at the base. Add the third and fourth small petals on opposite sides of this central core, stitching them in place in the same way.

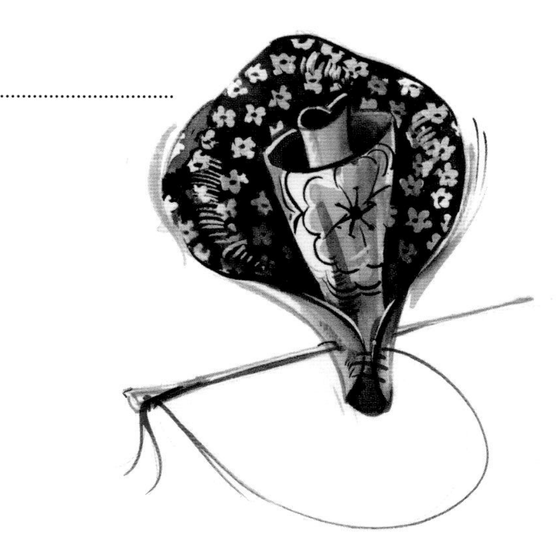

Adding the medium-size petals Now add the medium-size petals, one at a time, overlapping one over the other as you work around the centre. You may find you need to add a few extra stitches at the sides of the petals to keep the rose firmly in shape.

Adding the large petals Finally sew on the large petals, securing them at the base and sewing them to the wrong side of the previous round for 1–2cm from the base at each side.

Attaching the brooch back Stitch the brooch back, or a small safety pin, to the back of the corsage about 4cm from the outside edge.

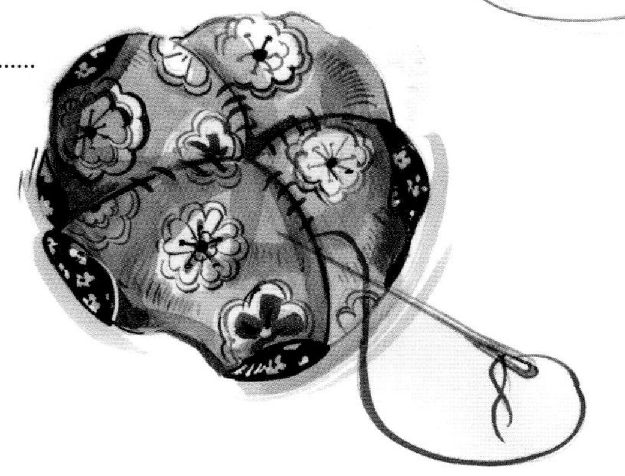

● FABRIC LEAVES WILL ADD A HIGHLIGHT OF COLOUR TO YOUR FINISHED CORSAGE. YOU CAN SNIP THESE FROM A SPRAY OF FABRIC FLOWERS OR LOOK OUT FOR MORE TEXTURED VELVET VERSIONS AT RIBBON STORES OR HABERDASHERS.

Rose Cushion

The spider-web embroidery used to create these naturalistic roses is usually worked with the narrowest of silk ribbons. I've taken the technique up to a much larger scale here and worked with torn strips of Liberty Tana Lawn to create densely packed, three-dimensional blooms in shades of pink, green and red. The cushion cover is backed with a rich velvet and a sprinkling of antique mother-of-pearl buttons adds to the luxurious, textured feel.

Finished size

47cm by 47cm

You will need

- For the cushion front, 50cm of velvet in red
- For the roses, 70cm of Liberty Tana Lawn, a lightweight cotton fabric, in each of a solid red, 'Pepper', 'Wiltshire' and 'Rock and Roll Rachel'
- For the cushion back, 50cm of crushed velvet in green
- Buttonhole or other strong thread, in colours to match roses fabrics
- Matching sewing thread
- Large crewel needle
- Large blunt-ended tapestry needle or bodkin
- 10 mother-of-pearl buttons with shanks (or large pearl beads)
- Cushion pad to fit finished cover

Cutting out

FROM RED VELVET:
Cut 1 cushion front 50cm square
FROM GREEN VELVET:
Cut 1 pillow back 50cm square
FROM ROSES FABRICS:
Tear 6cm strips as explained on page 98
NOTE: Seam allowance (1.5cm) is included in the cutting size.

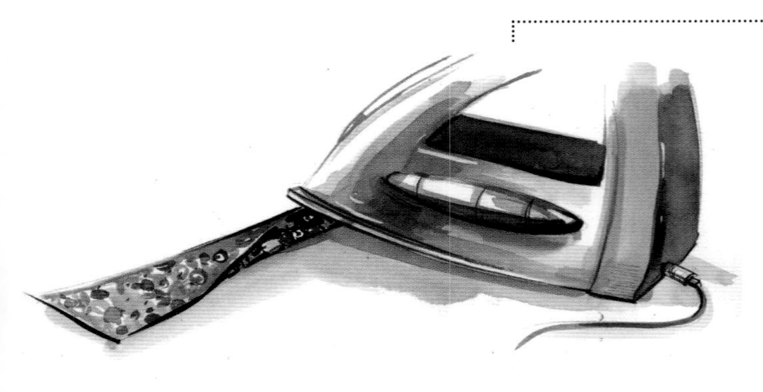

Preparing the fabric strips for the roses For each rose, tear a 6cm wide strip of fabric selvedge-to-selvedge from one of the four rose fabrics. Snip off any long loose threads, then press the strip in half lengthways with the wrong side facing inwards. If any of your print fabrics have a paler wrong side, press a few of these strips the other way round with the wrong sides facing outwards to obtain more colour variation in your roses. Prepare a few strips from each of the four rose fabrics to start. (Tear and press more strips only as you need them, so you won't end up tearing more strips than you need – you can save the surplus for other projects.)

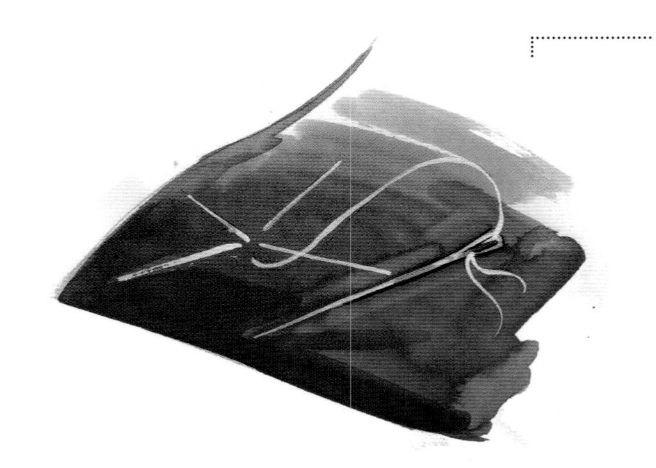

Starting a rose Starting at the bottom left corner of the velvet cushion front, work the foundation for the first rose. Using a double length of strong thread in a colour matching the rose and a large crewel needle, sew five long stitches radiating out from a centre point. Each stitch should be 4–5cm long but the length and arrangement doesn't have to be too precise – each rose is quite individual. Leave a margin of at least 1.5cm between the stitches and the edge of the fabric to allow space for the seam.

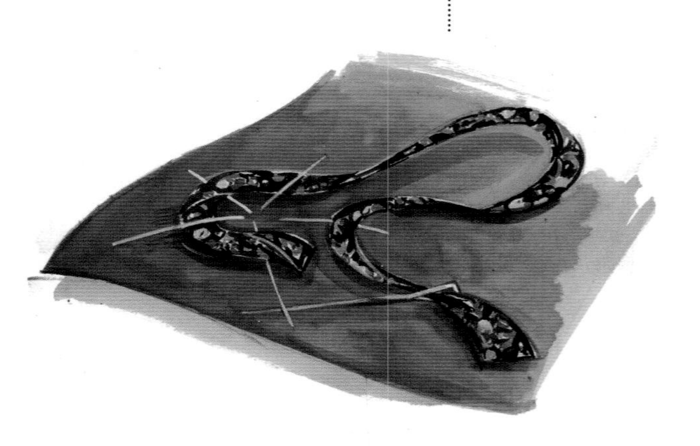

Weaving the rose strip around the base spokes Thread one end of the fabric through the eye of a large blunt-ended tapestry needle or bodkin. Sew the other end to the velvet cushion front, close to centre of the spokes, then weave the strip clockwise between them. Start by going over the first, under the second and then over the third, under the fourth and over the fifth. Pull up the fabric gently – it will turn back on itself to create the curled petal effect – then continue going round and round the spokes until only 5cm of the rose strip remains.

• CHOOSE A CUSHION PAD THAT IS LARGER THAN THE FINISHED COVER TO GIVE THE CUSHION A LUXURIOUSLY PLUMP LOOK.

Securing the end of the rose strip Make a tiny slit in the velvet at the end of final round, and take the needle through to the back. Sew the loose strip end in place on the wrong side of the cushion front so the flower cannot unravel.

Finishing the rose Stitch the edge of the outside petals to the cushion front, to keep them in shape, using an ordinary sewing needle and a matching sewing thread.

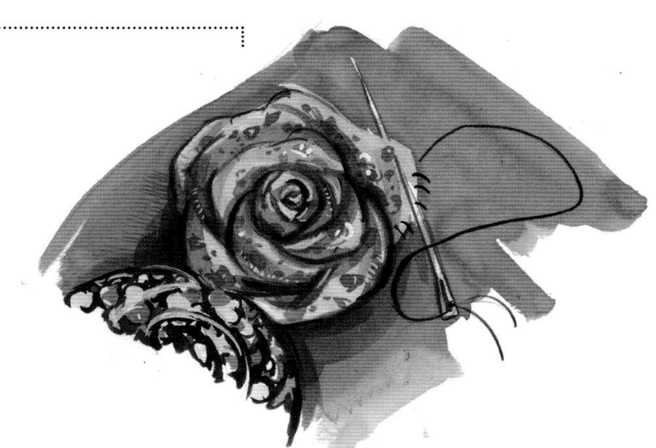

Adding the remaining roses Stitch five more roses close to each other along the bottom edge of the fabric. Then start the second row with a flower half the width of the full roses in the first row. Centre each of the next five roses in the second row between two roses in the first row – angling the spoke stitches into the space between the roses below – and end the row with another narrow flower. Continue making interlocking rows of roses until the cushion front is completely covered. Six rows of roses should fill the cushion front.

Adding the buttons (or large pearl beads) Add small highlights of colour by sewing mother-of-pearl buttons (or large pearl beads) to the centre of ten flowers, spreading them evenly across the front.

Finishing the cushion Turn back and tack down a 1.5cm turning along each edge of the cushion front. Do the same with the cushion back and then pin the two together with wrong sides together. Using a matching sewing thread, slipstitch the front and back together around three edges. Insert the cushion pad and pin the front to the back along the opening. Slipstitch the opening closed and remove the tacking.

● FOR EXTRA DEPTH AND VARIETY OF COLOUR TO THE CUSHION, ONE OF THE FABRICS WAS USED BOTH RIGHT SIDE AND WRONG SIDE UP FOR THE ROSES. THIS WORKS ESPECIALLY WELL WITH THE LIBERTY TANA LAWN 'ROCK AND ROLL RACHEL' PAISLEY PRINT, WHICH HAS A DUSKY ROSE TONE ON THE REVERSE.

Bench Cushion

This basic box, or welted, cushion can be adapted to create comfortable seating for any rectangular bench or window seat. Furnishing foam, cut to your own measurements, can be bought from specialist suppliers: ensure that it meets current safety standards before ordering. A calico under cover, made in the same way as the canvas cover, will prolong the life of the foam, and if you want a slightly softer look, add a layer of polyester wadding around the foam.

Finished size

Adjustable to fit your own bench seat

You will need

- Liberty Cotton Canvas in 'Pansies', a heavy-weight cotton furnishing fabric in a floral print
- Matching sewing thread
- Safety foam cushion, approximately 5.5cm thick, cut to the size of your seat

Measuring up

MAIN PANEL PIECES (top and bottom)

- width = width of foam cushion, plus 3cm
- length = length of foam cushion, plus 3cm

LONG SIDE GUSSETS

- width = depth of foam cushion, plus 3cm
- length = length of foam cushion, plus 3cm

SHORT SIDE GUSSETS

- width = depth of foam cushion, plus 3cm
- length = width of foam cushion, plus 3cm

NOTE: If you are making a cushion for a square seat, the gussets will all be the same length. For a rectangular seat you need two short and two long gussets.

Cutting out

- Cut 2 main panel pieces
- Cut 2 long gussets
- Cut 2 short gussets

Marking the seam lines Using a sharp pencil, mark a point at each corner of each of the six fabric pieces, 1.5cm in from the side edges. Do this on the wrong side for the gussets and the right side for the main pieces (using a light coloured pencil on dark fabric if necessary). These marked dots indicate where the seam lines begin and end.

Pinning the gusset Press under and then unfold a 1.5cm turning along one long edge of one of the long gusset pieces – this will be the opening. With right sides together, pin a short gusset piece to each end of this long gusset piece, then pin the other long gusset piece to the short gusset pieces to make a long loop of fabric.

Joining the gusset pieces together Machine stitch the four gusset pieces together with a 1.5cm seam allowance, sewing between the dots. You will need to reinforce the ends of each line of stitching with a few reverse stitches. Press the seams open.

Pinning the gusset to the first main panel Again with right sides together, pin the raw edges of the gusset loop to one of the main panel pieces, with the long gusset edge with the pressed-under seam allowance pointing upwards. Open out the seams at the corners so that they stand up at right angles and match the ends of the seams to the dots.

• THERE ARE MANY SPECIALIST SUPPLIERS WHO CAN CUT FOAM TO SIZE.

Joining the gusset to the first main panel With the gusset upwards, machine stitch all around the main piece, 1.5cm from the edge.

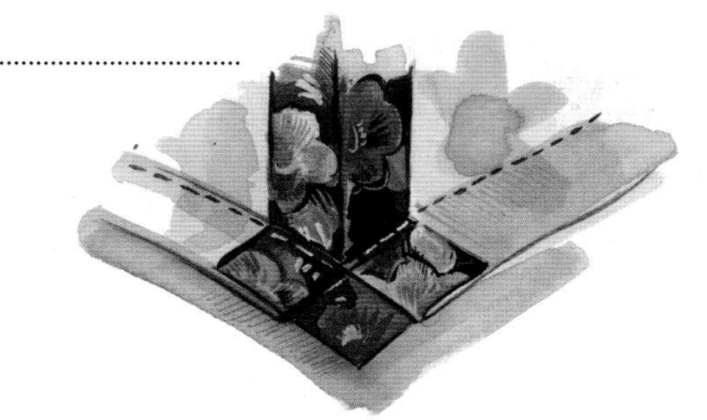

Joining the gusset to the second main panel Press under a 1.5cm turning along one long edge of the second main panel piece: this will be the other side of the opening. Pin the short edges and the other long edge to the gusset, as before, matching the turned edge to the turned gusset edge. Machine stitch the three edges with a 1.5cm seam allowance, leaving the open edge unstitched.

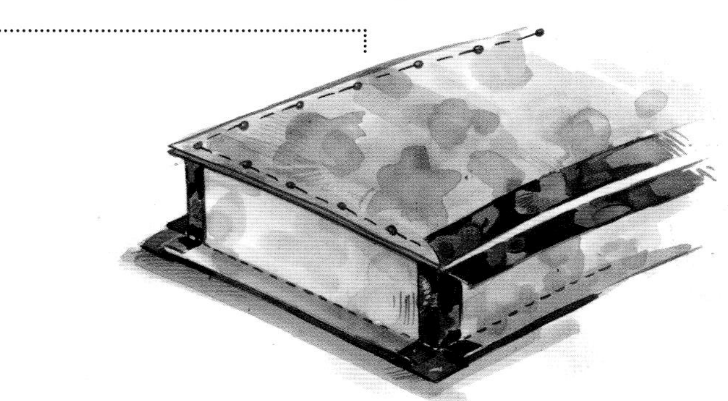

Trimming the corner seam allowance Trim two thin triangles from the seam allowance of the main panel corners, snipping 3mm from the seam line. This reduces the amount of fabric and will give the finished cushion sharp corners. Turn the cover right side out, and press the seams. Insert the cushion through the opening – depending on the size of your bench, this might be tricky.

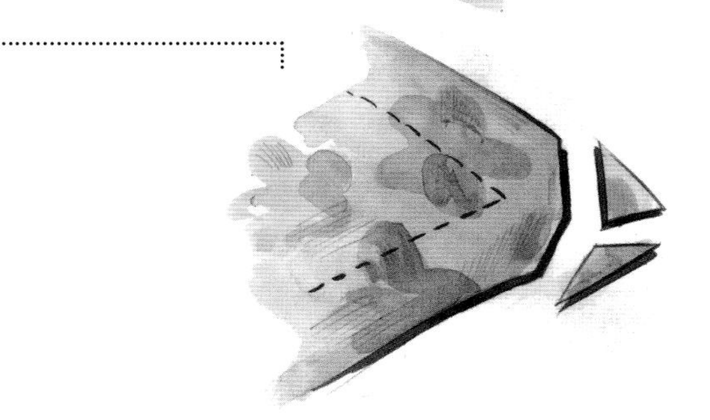

Finishing the cushion cover Check that the seam allowances are all lying flat against the foam pad – if they are twisted, the cushion will look lumpy. Along the opening, fold the seam allowance of the main piece over the edge of the foam cushion and pin the gusset down over it, so that the pressed folds meet up. Sew the gusset to the main panel with small, neat hand stitches.

- STOP YOUR CUSHION FROM SLIDING ABOUT BY SEWING ON COTTON TAPE OR FABRIC TIES THAT CAN BE SECURED TO THE BENCH LEGS. FOR A MORE MINIMALIST LOOK, USE LENGTHS OF HEAVY DUTY DOUBLE-SIDED CARPET OR RUG TAPE TO KEEP IT IN PLACE.

Frilly Pinny with Potholder

A touch of old-fashioned glamour never goes amiss, so take your cue from the not-so-desperate housewives of the 1950s and run up a frilly pinny for yourself or your best friend. Kitchen chores are a breeze when you are clad in Liberty Tana Lawn roses! To complete the look, button a handy potholder to the waistband in true vintage American style.

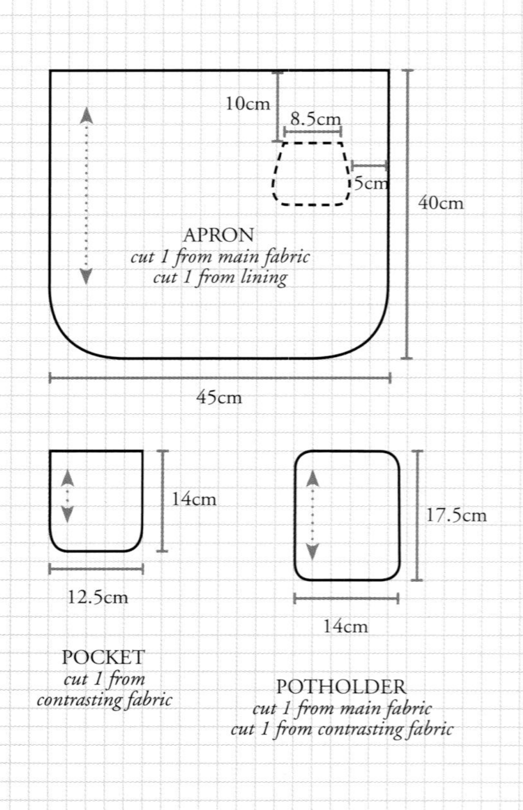

Finished size

43cm wide and 38cm long from waistband, excluding 9cm frill

You will need

- For contrasting fabric, 60cm of 136cm wide Liberty Tana Lawn in 'Glenjade', a lightweight cotton fabric in a mini print
- For main fabric, 45cm of Liberty Tana Lawn in 'Carline', a medium-scale floral print
- 45 x 50cm piece of a lightweight white cotton fabric, for lining
- Matching sewing thread
- Quilting thread, for hand gathering

Cutting out

FROM MAIN FABRIC:

- Cut 1 apron piece

FROM CONTRASTING FABRIC:

- Cut 1 pocket piece
- For frill and tie, cut 3 strips each 12 x 136cm, cutting selvedge-to-selvedge and retaining the selvedge edges

FROM LINING FABRIC:

- Cut 1 apron piece

EACH SQUARE = 2.5cm
NOTE: SEAM ALLOWANCE IS INCLUDED IN PATTERN-PIECE SIZE.

Marking out the frill position Using a tape measure as a guide, insert a line of pins at 5cm intervals all the way around the side and bottom edges of the apron – this divides the apron edge into 23 equal sections. These guide pins ensure the frill is distributed evenly.

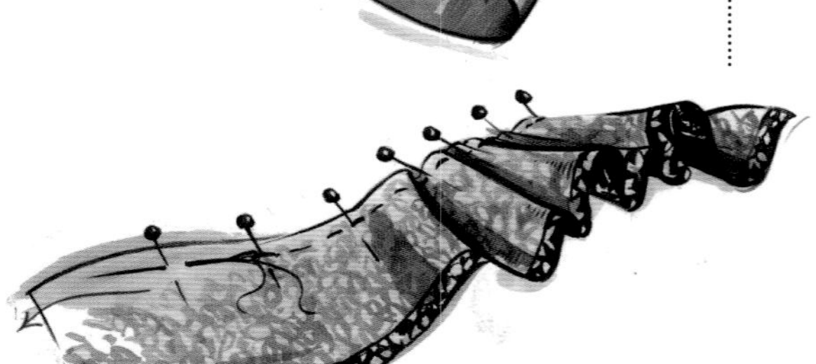

Preparing the frill Pin the three 12 x 137cm strips together end-to-end, with right sides together, and machine stitch with 1.5cm seams. Press the seams open. Cut a 230cm strip from one end of the long joined strip for the frill (set aside the remaining strip for the apron waistband tie). Fold back and press 1cm twice along one long edge of the frill piece to form a double hem and machine stitch. Now with the wrong side upwards, divide the frill into 23 equal sections by placing a pin every 10cm along the raw edge. Thread a needle with a long length of quilting thread and sew a line of long running stitches all the way along the frill 1cm from the raw edge. Pull up the thread as you go so that the gap between the pins is reduced to roughly 5cm.

Stitching the frill to the apron Pin the frill to the apron, with right sides together. Start at the top left corner of the apron and match up the two sets of pins. You may need to adjust each section of gathers so that they are spaced evenly – do this by using the tip of a pin to move the fabric along the thread. Machine stitch over the gathering thread to stabilise the frill.

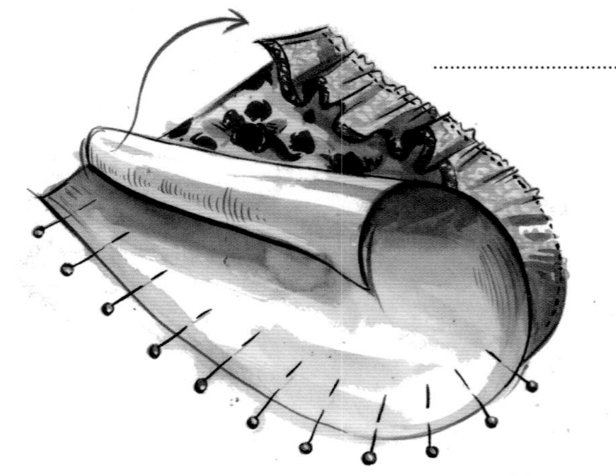

Adding the lining Pin the lining to the front of the apron along the side and bottom edges, so that the frill is sandwiched between the two layers. With the floral fabric uppermost, machine stitch it to the lining, just inside the line of stabilising stitches. Trim the seam allowance back to 6mm and turn right side out. Press lightly along the seam line. Press lightly along the seam line.

● THE FABRICS USED TO MAKE THE APRON HAVE PATTERNS ON DIFFERENT SCALES, BUT THEY WORK WELL TOGETHER. A PLAIN TRIM WOULD WORK WELL TOO: PICK A COLOUR TO MATCH THE MAIN APRON OR GO FOR A MISMATCHED CONTRAST.

Adding the waistband ties Gather the top edge of the apron by sewing a line of running stitches through both layers, 6mm from the edge, and pulling it up to 30cm. Secure the end of the thread. Fold the apron in half widthways, and mark the centre of the waist with a pin. Press back a 1cm turning along one long edge of the waistband tie, then unfold the crease. Find the centre of the waistband tie along the creased edge and, with right sides facing and raw edges lined up, pin the centre of the waistband tie to the centre of the top of the apron. Now pin the apron to the waistband from the center out to the right corner, making sure the gathers lie evenly between the pins. Pin the edge of the frill to the band. Pin the left sides together in the same way. Machine stitch along the top edge of the apron and frills, 1cm from the raw edge.

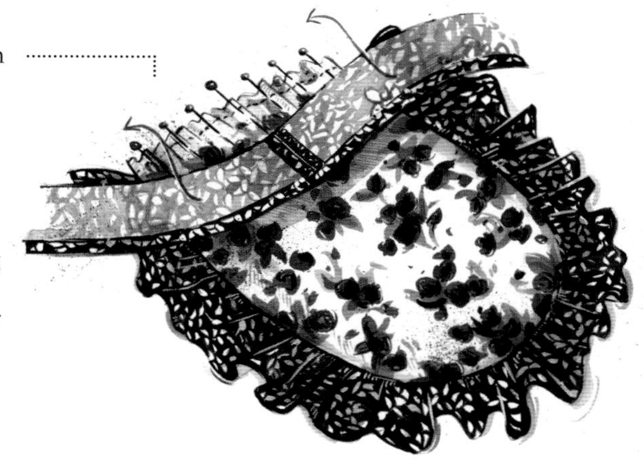

Pressing under the edges on the waistband ties Press under a 1cm turning along the other long edge of the waistband tie. (Adjust the length of the tie now if necessary.) Press under 1cm along each short end of the tie, then press the band in half along the entire length so there is a centre crease. Fold the corners at each end to the centre crease and press. This will give a neatly pointed end to the ties.

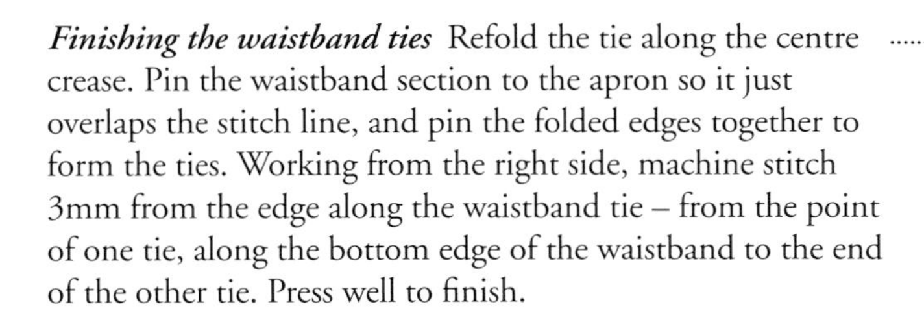

Finishing the waistband ties Refold the tie along the centre crease. Pin the waistband section to the apron so it just overlaps the stitch line, and pin the folded edges together to form the ties. Working from the right side, machine stitch 3mm from the edge along the waistband tie – from the point of one tie, along the bottom edge of the waistband to the end of the other tie. Press well to finish.

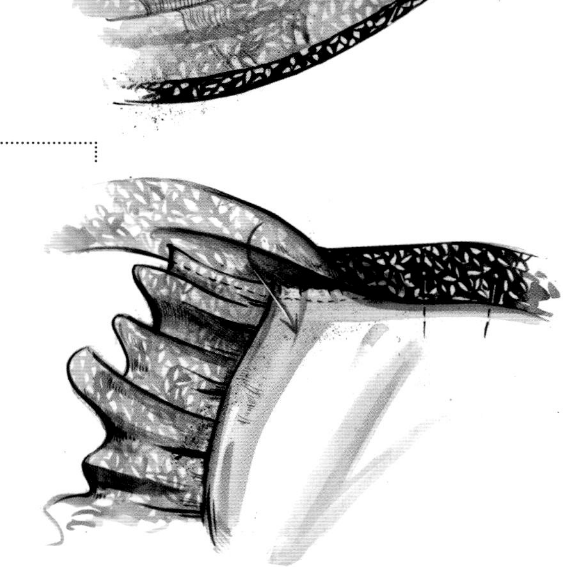

Adding the pocket Press under a 1cm turning along the sides, curved corners, and bottom of the pocket. Fold back and press 1cm twice along the pocket top to form a double hem. Machine stitch the top hem 3mm from the edge. Pin the pocket to the top right corner of the apron, sloping each side in by 1cm – this will give it a puffed-out look. Machine stitch in place, 3mm from the fold.

Taking it further – potholder

The perfect finishing touch for any apron just has to be a coordinating quilted potholder.

Finished size

14cm by 17.5cm

You will need

- Main and contrasting fabric leftover from apron
- 20 x 25cm piece of quilt wadding
- 80cm of 12mm wide cotton bias binding
- One 2cm decorative button
- Matching sewing thread
- Ruler or quilter's square

Cutting out

FROM MAIN FABRIC, CONTRASTING FABRIC AND WADDING

- Cut 1 rectangular 20 x 25cm

NOTE: Once the three rectangles are quilted together, they are cut to the shape of the potholder using the pattern piece on page 106.

1 Using a ruler or quilter's square and a sharp pencil, draw a 3cm grid diagonally across the right side of the main fabric piece. Place the contrasting fabric piece face downwards, then the wadding with the main fabric on top, face upwards. Pin and tack the three layers together around the edge, then diagonally from corner to corner.

2 Machine stitch along each of the pencil grid lines. Make a paper template of the potholder pattern piece with the curved corners (see page 106), pin it to the finished piece of quilting and cut out. Remove the tacking.

3 Bind the edge of the potholder with cotton bias binding, starting the round at the centre top edge. You can see how to do this – by hand or by machine – on page 149. To make the hanging loop, cut an 8cm length from the remaining bias binding. Press under 6mm at each end, then stitch the two folded edges together. Sew the ends over the join in the binding. Sew the button to the apron waistband and loop the potholder onto it.

Kimono

Add a touch of old-fashioned glamour to your daily routine with this slinky wrap-around robe, which combines two richly-hued abstract Liberty prints in different textures: 'Bailando en Mis Suenos' Balcombe Silk, trimmed with another silk, 'Combe' Harcourt Crepe de Chine. It is a comfortable UK size 12, which finishes at mid-calf. Hold the pattern against you before cutting out the fabric, to double check the length and adjust it as necessary for a longer or shorter version. Remember that you will need more fabric for a full-length kimono.

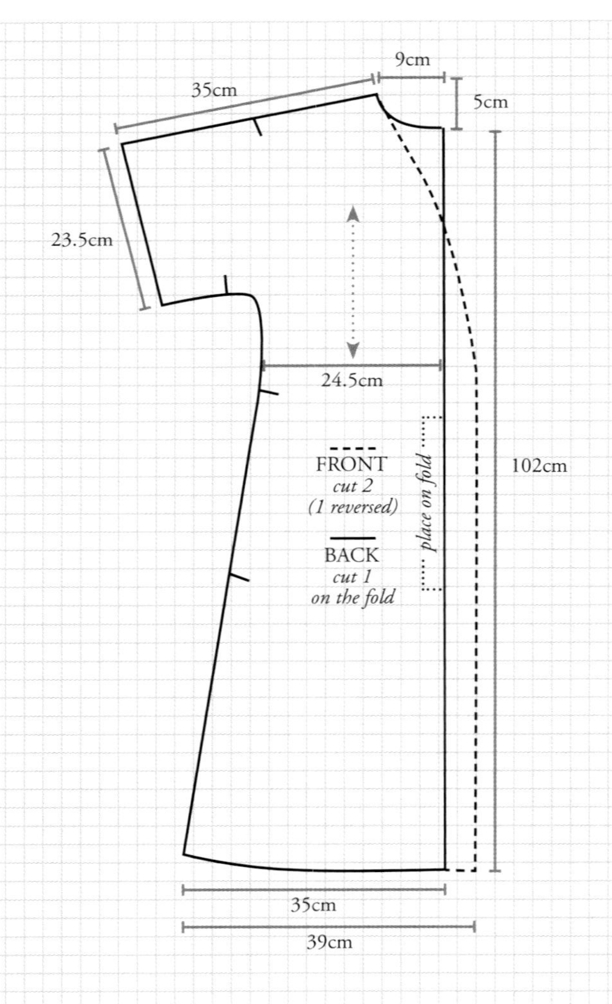

Finished size

Size 12, with mid-calf length

You will need

- For main fabric, 2.2m of Liberty Balcombe Silk in 'Bailando En Mis Suenos', a lightweight silk satin in a large-scale print
- For contrasting fabric, 1.1m of Liberty Harcourt Crepe de Chine in 'Combe', a lightweight silk crepe de chine in a large-scale print
- Matching sewing thread
- Dressmaker's pattern paper

EACH SQUARE = 2.5cm
NOTE: SEAM ALLOWANCE (1.5cm) IS INCLUDED IN PATTERN-PIECE SIZE.

Cutting out

Make a paper pattern piece of all the pieces needed for the kimono, including the rectangles for the front band, cuff, belt and belt loop, and use these to cut the fabric pieces. Transfer all markings onto your pattern pieces. Cut all pieces on straight grain of fabric except where instructed otherwise.

FROM MAIN FABRIC:

- Cut 1 back, on the fold
- Cut 2 fronts (1 reversed)

FROM CONTRASTING FABRIC:

- Cut 2 front bands, on the bias, each 11 x 127cm
- Cut 2 cuffs, on the bias, each 11 x 44cm
- Cut 2 belt pieces, each 11 x 66cm
- Cut 2 belt loops, on the bias, each 3.5 x 15cm

NOTE: Cut one or two 5mm slits into the seam allowance at each of the points marked on the pattern: these will help you line up the pieces exactly when you pin them together.

Neatening the raw edges of the front and back pieces
Set your sewing machine to a large zigzag stitch or other overlocking stitch. Using matching sewing thread, machine stitch along each of the shoulder and underarm/ side edges of the front and back pieces.

Making the belt loops Following the technique instructions on page 67 for the jewellery roll ties, make the two belt loops into rouleaux. Fold them in half and pin to the back piece on the marked waistline matching the raw edges. (Check first that the waist in the right position for you, and adjust as necessary.)

Stitching the front and back pieces together With right sides together, pin the two front pieces to the back, matching the notches in the seam allowance. Machine stitch together, leaving a 1.5cm seam allowance.

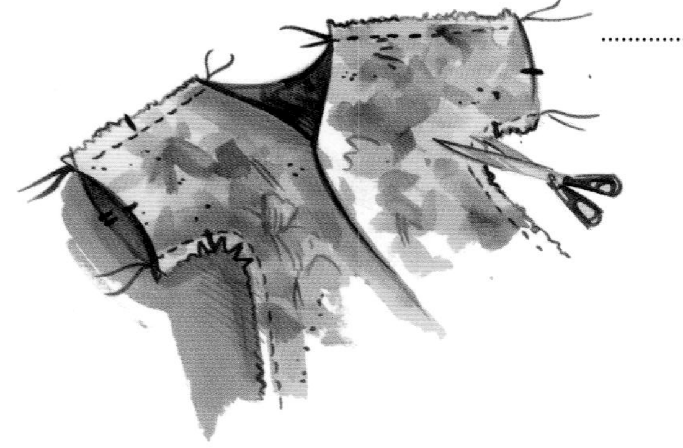

Clipping the curved seams Work a second line of machine stitching over the first to reinforce the curved part of the underarm seam. Cut three or four small notches into the seam allowance here so that it will lie flat. Press all of the seams open and turn the kimono right side out.

Preparing the cuffs Pin the short ends of the cuffs together, with right sides facing and machine stitch 1.5cm from the edge. Press the seams open, then press back a 1.5cm turning around the outside edge.

Stitching on the cuffs With right sides together, pin the cuffs to the sleeves, matching the seams to the underarm seams. Machine stitch, 1.5cm from the edge, then trim the seam allowance to 1cm. Press the seam allowances towards the cuffs.

Finishing the cuffs Turn the kimono wrong side out and fold the cuffs in half so that the folded edges lie along the stitched lines, concealing the seam allowance. Pin in place and slipstitch the fold to the seam allowance, as close as possible to the stitching.

Turning up the hem Press a 1cm turning along the bottom edge of the kimono, then press under 3cm more. Pin in place, and hand or machine stitch down, easing in any extra fullness. Tack the raw edges together at the ends of the hem.

Stitching the front bands together Pin and stitch the two front band pieces together end to end: this seam will lie at the centre back. Press the seam open, then press a 1.5cm turning all the way along one long edge.

Adding the front band With right sides together, pin the band seam line to the kimono centre back. Pin each edge out to the bottom corners of the two front pieces. The two ends will hang below the hem. Machine stitch, leaving a 1.5cm seam allowance. Press the seam outwards, towards the band. Press under the two ends of the front band so that they are in line with the hem.

Finishing the front band Fold the band to the inside of the kimono so that the long folded edge is lined up to the seam line. You will need to ease it around curved edges of the two front pieces. Pin in place and stitch down by hand or machine. Slipstitch the bottom edges of the facing together on the left and right fronts.

Making the belt With right sides together, pin and stitch the two belt pieces together and press the seam open. Fold the belt in half lengthways with right sides together. Pin, then stitch together 1cm from the edge, leaving an opening of approximately 15cm near the centre seam. Clip the corners, then turn right side out through this opening. Press flat and slipstitch the opening closed.

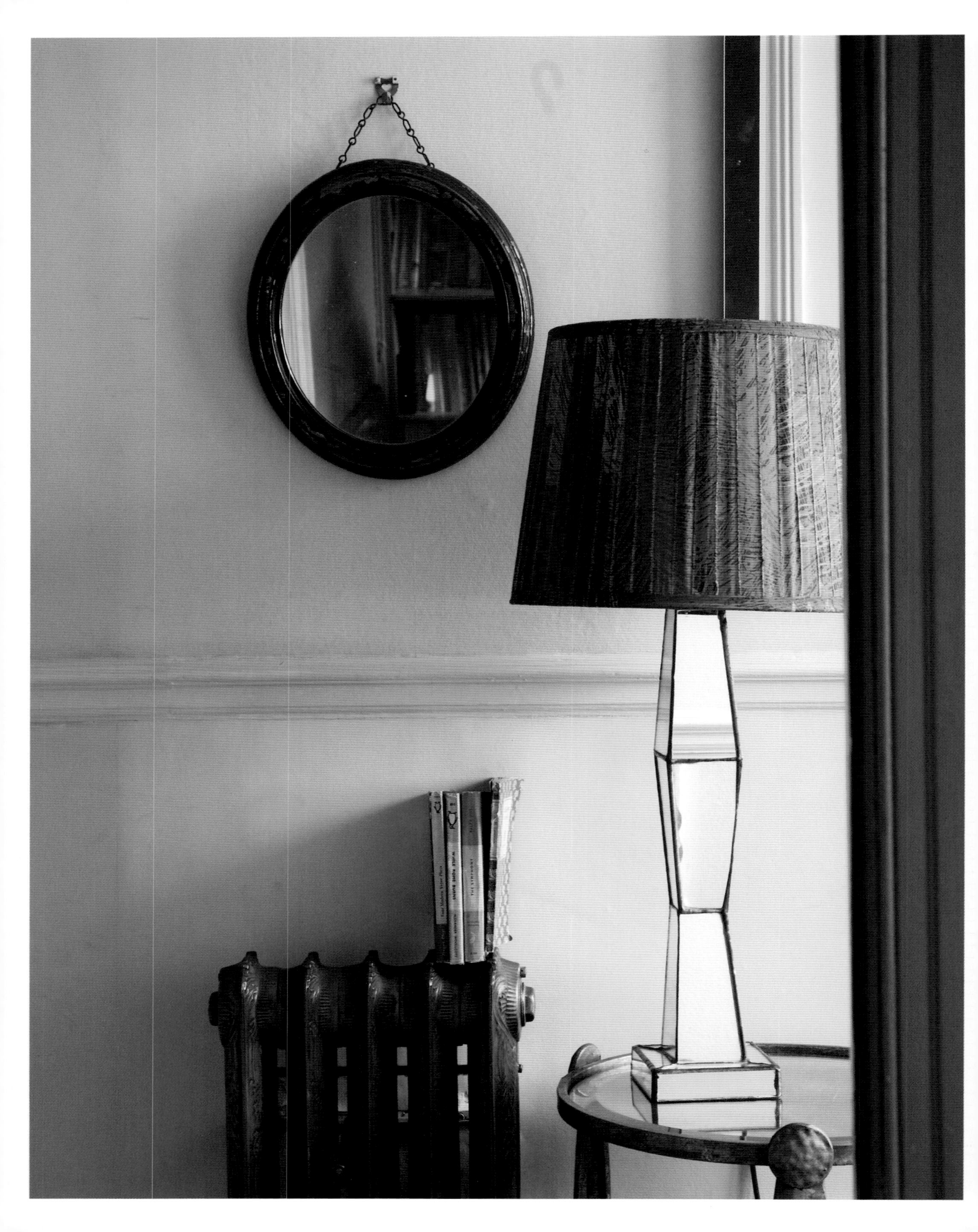
WHILE ROME BURNS
THE SYMPHONY

Lampshade

There seems to be a real gap in the interiors market for fabulous lampshades, which provides the perfect excuse to have a go at making one yourself. You can buy a new metal frame from a specialist supplier, recycle your existing shades or revamp a flea market find in a fabric that matches your design scheme. This project is very quick to execute and only the most basic of sewing skills are needed.

Finished size

Covering to fit any size lampshade

You will need

- Liberty Tana Lawn in 'Explosions in the Sky', a lightweight cotton fabric (see Measuring up for fabric amount)
- Matching sewing thread
- 2cm wide double-sided cellophane tape

Measuring up

The amount of fabric needed will vary depending on how closely you bind the strips and on the size of the lampshade. As a guide, this frame – 36cm in diameter and 30cm tall – took approximately 90cm of fabric torn into 4cm strips.

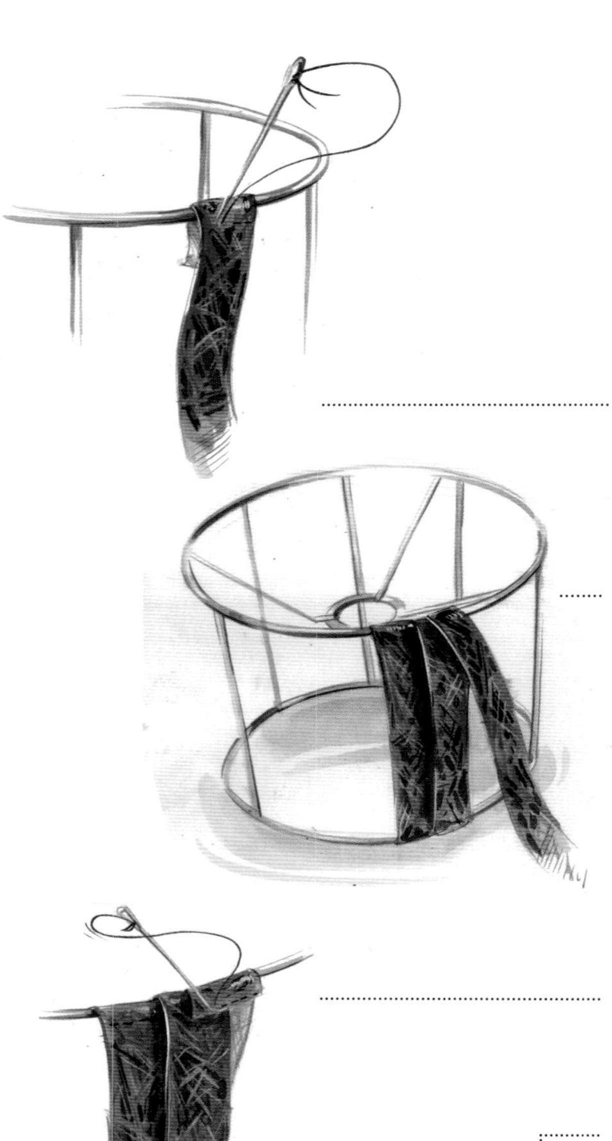

Preparing the fabric Trim the selvedges from both side edges of the fabric. Then begin to tear the fabric selvedge-to-selvedge into 4cm wide strips. Once you have about ten strips, remove any loose threads and press the strips flat. (Tear and press more strips only as you need them, so you won't end up tearing more strips than you need – you can save the surplus for other projects.)

Starting off a strip Fold the end of the first strip over the top ring of the metal lampshade frame and secure the end in place with a few stab stitches.

Winding the first strip around the frame Take the strip down over the outisde of the bottom ring of the frame, then inside the frame and back up over the top. Continue winding the strip around the frame from left to right, overlapping each round by about 1.5cm.

Starting a new strip When you finish winding the first strip, trim it back so that the end overlaps the nearest edge by 1cm. Stitch the end down, then sew on the next strip at the same point and continue binding. (Make sure you always end and start strips along the top or bottom edges of the frame, where they will be concealed by the binding.)

Working around the struts When you reach the first horizontal strut at the top of the metal frame, make a small slit in the right edge of the fabric so that it will fit around the strut. Cut the left edge of the fabric when you bring it back up, so that it fits around the other side of the strut.

Securing the strips in place Continue until you have encircled the entire frame. Then work a round of small running stitches through both layers of strips at the top and bottom of the frame, close to the metal rings. These stitches will hold the strips securely in place.

Binding the edges The top and bottom edges of the frame are finished off with a fabric binding, fixed in place with double-sided tape. Cut (or tear) two 5cm wide selvedge-to-selvedge strips of fabric, one for the top and one for the bottom. (If the strips are not long enough to encircle your frame, stitch two strips together and press the seam open.) Press under a 1cm turning along each long edge of one strip then adhere a length of double-sided tape down the center of the wrong side of the strip, over the hems. Stick the tape around the top edge of the frame, peeling off the paper backing little by little as you proceed. Make small slits on the inside edge to accommodate the horizontal struts and overlap the ends by 3cm. Do the same at the bottom edge. (See the Safety First tip below.)

Taking it further

The splashy red 'Explosions in the Sky' print is sophisticated enough for any living space, but you may prefer a softer design such as 'Miranda' to go in a bedroom or playroom. To get an idea of how a fabric will look when torn and bound, fold it into random pleats and see how the patterns overlap. The results will always be surprising.

● SAFETY FIRST DON'T FORGET THAT FABRIC SHADES SHOULD ALWAYS BE USED WITH A LOW WATTAGE ENERGY-SAVING LIGHT-BULB, WHICH EMITS A LOW LEVEL OF HEAT.

Rose Throw

The 'broderie perse' technique evolved in the eighteenth century, when precious fragments of printed Indian fabrics were brought to Europe. This appliqué method was used to make the fragments go a long way and to preserve them. With its large, splashy flowers, 'Kate Ada' is perfect for this technique. Use the flower print motifs with solid-coloured cotton motifs to give a paper-cut look.

Finished size

111cm wide by 131cm long

You will need

- For throw front, 125cm of off-white linen or similar heavy-weight fabric
- For throw borders, 125cm of Liberty Tana Lawn in solid red, a lightweight cotton fabric
- For floral print motifs, 90cm of Liberty Tana Lawn in 'Kate Ada', a large-scale floral print
- For solid-colour motifs, 25cm of Liberty Tana Lawn in each of two solid colours
- For backing, 1.4m of Liberty Tana Lawn in a small-scale print
- Matching sewing thread
- 90cm of fusible adhesive bonding web
- Two or more bright contrasting coloured sewing threads, for embroidery on appliqué

Cutting out

FROM LINEN:

- Cut 1 throw front piece 102 x 122cm

FROM SOLID-COLOURED BORDER FABRIC:

- Cut 2 side border strips, each 9 x 122cm
- Cut top and bottom border strips, each 9 x 114cm

FROM BACKING FABRIC PRINT:

- Cut 1 backing piece 114 x 134cm

FROM LARGE-SCALE FLORAL PRINT AND REMAINING SOLID COLOUR:

- Cut motifs as directed on page 124

NOTE: Seam allowance (1.5cm) is included in the cutting size.

Cutting out the motifs Following the manufacturer's instructions, iron the fusible adhesive bonding web to wrong side of your large-scale floral print and roughly cut out a variety of printed motifs: single blooms of various sizes, flowers with attached leaves, and single leaves. (As an example, the throw pictured has 5 small, 11 medium-size and 5 large flowers.) Trim all the motifs to shape, following the outline carefully but not too precisely. Make a few with one flat side to place around the edges.

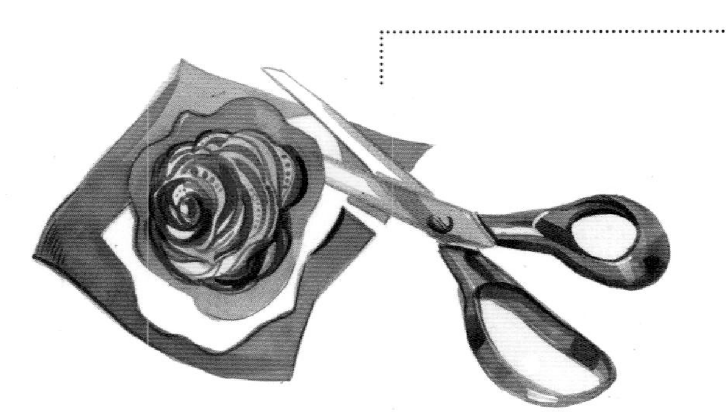

Preparing flower motifs with solid-coloured backings Mount some of the flower motifs on the solid-coloured fabrics to increase their size and add extra colour emphasis. (Use the remnants of the left-over border fabric and the other two solid colours for these backings.) Press a piece of fusible adhesive bonding web to a piece of fabric that is about 2cm larger all round than the flower. Peel the backing paper from the flower motif and fuse centrally to the solid-coloured backing, then cut out with a curving, flowing line.

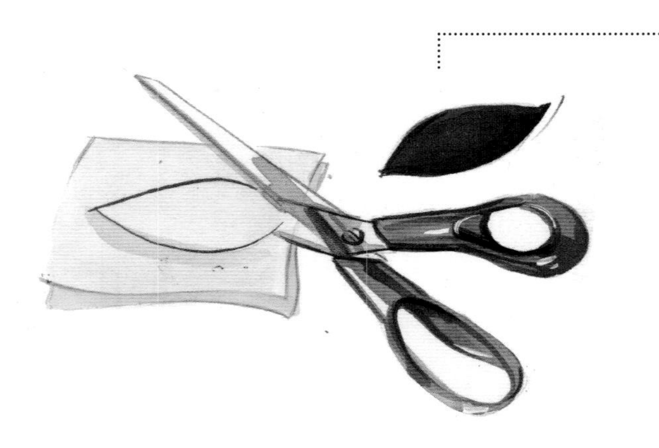

Cutting out the extra solid-coloured leaves Finally, make extra plain leaves from the remaining scraps of the three solid colours. (There are 32 of these extra leaves on the throw pictured.) For each motif, draw a tapered leaf shape on the paper side of the bonding web and iron it to fabric. Cut out around the pencil line.

Positioning the motifs Lay the flowers and leaves across the throw front piece, rearranging them until you are pleased with the design. Space them evenly, with the flat-sided shapes at the edges. Peel off all the backing papers, tuck the single leaves under the flowers and pin the pieces in place.

Fusing the motifs to the throw Use a hot dry iron to fuse the motifs to the throw, following the manufacturer's instructions. For multilayered motifs, press on the leaves first, then add the flower to cover the ends.

Adding the machine embroidery Each motif is stitched down with flowing lines of straight stitch. If you haven't 'drawn' with your sewing machine before, then practise on a fabric scrap. The outlines around the flowers should be very fluid, and like the veins on the leaves. The embroidery lines can extend beyond the edge of the motifs. Use bright, contrasting sewing thread in two or more shades.

Anselm Kiefer
WILLIAM MORRIS by himself
LUCIAN FREUD
The School of London
Banksy
CHAIM SOUTINE
IMPRESSIONISM
HERBERT
PAULA
Marlene Dumas
CEZANNE by himself
Andy Goldsworthy
TIME

Joining on the borders Pin the two long border strips to the side edges of the appliquéd throw, with right sides together, and stitch together with a 1.5cm seam allowance. Press the seams outwards, so that they lie under the borders. Add the short border strips to the top and bottom edges in the same way.

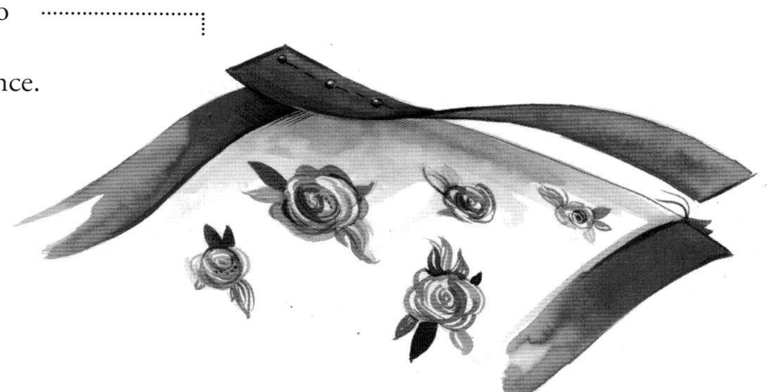

Adding the backing With right sides together, pin the backing to the throw front around the outside edge. Machine stitch with a 1.5cm seam allowance, leaving a 30cm opening in the middle of one side for turning through. Press back the seam allowance on each side of the opening. Clip a small triangle from each corner (see page 151) and turn the throw right side out. Ease out the corners and press lightly from the wrong side. Pin the folded edges of the opening together and slipstitch closed.

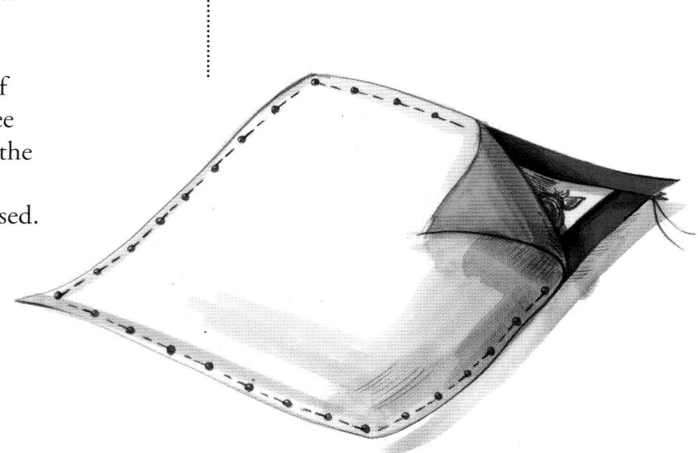

● THE FLORAL MOTIFS COULD BE HAND STITCHED ON TO THE THROW, IF PREFERRED. USE BUTTONHOLE STITCHES WITH RUNNING STITCHES FOR THE EMBROIDERED OUTLINES.

Traditional Cot Quilt

Traditional hexagon patchwork has a timeless charm of its own, which makes this 'Grandmother's Flower Garden' quilt the perfect showcase for a selection of classic Liberty Tana Lawns. Each of the six-petalled rosettes is made up of two floral prints, chosen to contrast in both colour and scale. The quilt is stitched entirely by hand using the English technique of sewing over foundation papers, so making it – over many hours – will be a true labour of love.

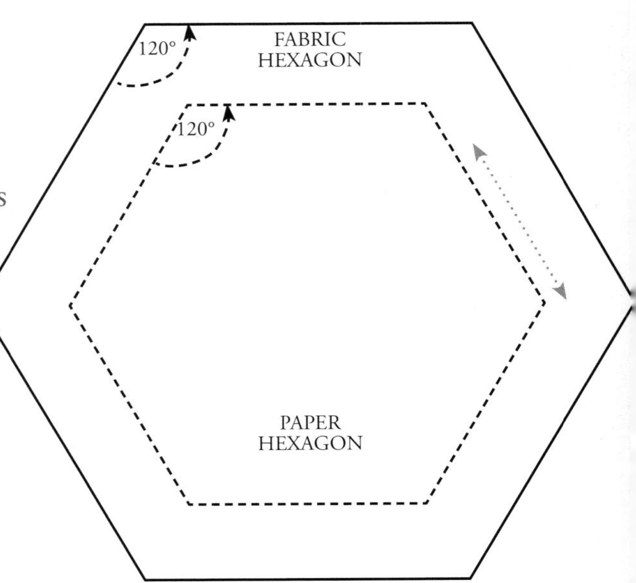

Finished size

83cm wide by 126.5cm long, to fit a child's cot (see Altering Quilt Size)

You will need

- For floral hexagons, 20cm of Liberty Tana Lawn in 'Capel', 'Douglas Stripe', 'Eloise', 'Fairford', 'Pepper', 'Rania', 'Sarah's Secret Garden' and 'Tatum', a lightweight cotton fabric in eight different small-scale and mini floral prints
- For white hexagons, 90cm of a 112cm wide lightweight white cotton fabric
- For backing, 1.4m of a 112cm wide lightweight white cotton fabric
- Thick polyester quilt wadding, 95 x 137cm
- Matching sewing thread
- Quilting thread, in white
- Thin, stiff cardboard, for templates
- Recycled paper – such as old envelopes – for the backing papers
- Block of beeswax (optional)
- Safety pins (optional)

Altering quilt size

The instructions are for a quilt for a small child. To make a version for a single, double or even king-sized bed, increase the amount of materials proportionately.

Cutting out

Cut out the fabric hexagons as explained below to make 25 full six-petaled floral-print rosettes and six four-petaled floral-print half rosettes. The total number of hexagons required for the cot quilt are given below.

FROM FLORAL HEXAGON FABRIC:

- Cut a total of 205 hexagons – to approximate this amount, cut 26 hexagons from each of the eight prints, for a total of 208 hexagons

FROM WHITE HEXAGON FABRIC:

- Cut 168 white hexagons

FROM BACKING FABRIC:

- Cut backing to same size as quilt wadding, 95 x 137cm

CUTTING THE FABRIC HEXAGONS Trace the templates onto thin cardboard, then cut around the outlines. Using a sharp pencil, draw around the smaller template to make a stack of backing papers from recycled paper – you need a total of 373 backing papers. To cut a fabric hexagon, draw around the larger template onto the wrong side of the fabric. Alternatively pin a backing paper to the fabric and cut out a fabric shape 1cm larger all around than the paper. The fabric hexagon size doesn't have to be accurate, just big enough to overlap onto the backing paper. Using the cutting template avoids wastage as you can trace the hexagons onto the fabric with the edges abutting.

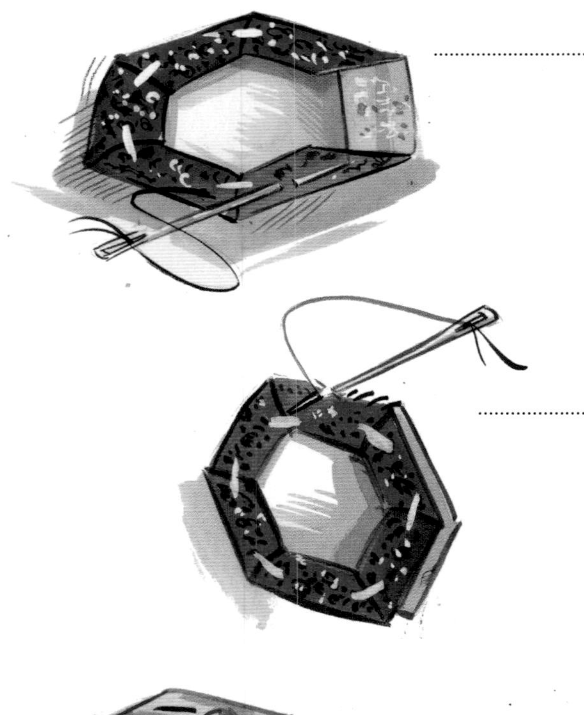

Preparing the hexagon patches To prepare each patch, hold a backing paper centrally against the wrong side of the fabric, then fold back each edge, fingerpressing as you proceed, and tack down each of the sides one at a time. Stitch right through the paper and make a neat 120-degree angle at each point. Each rosette is made up of six matching floral fabric 'petals' around a contrasting centre, so to make the first rosette prepare at least six matching hexagons and one contrasting hexagon. Prepare the remaining sets of patches as you need them.

Starting a hexagon rosette Place the first of the six matching petals over the contrasting central hexagon, with right sides together. Thread a short, fine needle with matching sewing cotton and knot the end (use white thread if your floral print has a white ground). Slide the needle under the turned-back fabric and bring it through at the top right corner of the first petal. Overcast stitch the two patches together along the top edge with small, regular stitches. Slip the needle through the folded fabric on both sides as you sew, and secure the end of the seam with a few extra stitches, worked in the opposite direction.

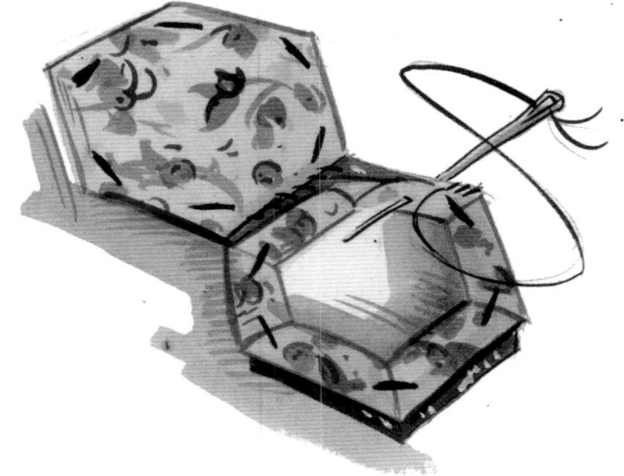

Sewing the second petal to the rosette centre Open out the two patches and stitch the second petal to the next side of the centre hexagon.

Sewing the second petal to the first Now fold the centre hexagon in half so that the two petals lie face to face. Bring the needle up at the point where all three patches meet and stitch the two petals together.

• THE FINISHED QUILT MEASURES 83 X 126.5CM AND IS INTENDED FOR A SMALL CHILD: INCREASE THE AMOUNT OF MATERIALS PROPORTIONATELY TO MAKE A VERSION FOR A SINGLE, DOUBLE OR EVEN KING-SIZED BED.

Sewing on the remaining petals Sew on the remaining four petals in the same way to make the first rosette. You need 25 complete rosettes and 6 part rosettes (with four petals) for a quilt the size of the one shown here.

Preparing the background white hexagons When all the rosettes are complete, prepare the 168 white hexagons and set them aside.

Planning the quilt layout Arrange the rosettes in seven rows, starting with the top row of four, then alternating lines of three and four until you reach the bottom row of four. Position the part rosettes at each end of the rows of three. When you are satisfied with the balance of pattern and colour, number the back of each rosette, so you can rejoin them in the right order. Then arrange the white background hexagons all around the rosettes. (It's useful to take a photo of the final arrangement.)

Sewing on the background hexagons around the rosettes Sew 12 white hexagons around one rosette at the top of the quilt.

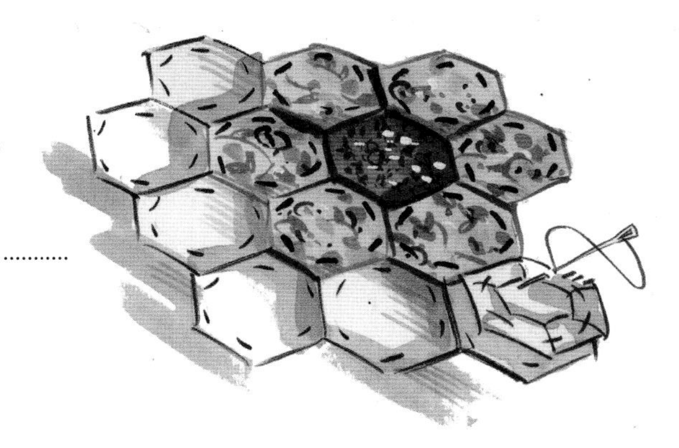

Sewing the rosettes together in rows Add the next rosette bordered with nine white hexagons to the first bordered rosette. You can sew the hexagons together in horizontal rows or diagonal rows (as shown here, with the corner rosette being sewn to the diagonal row next to it), but start at the top of the quilt. Complete your first row of rosettes, then sew on the rest, a row at a time. This will take a while, but remember that quilt making is a relaxing, unhurried process.

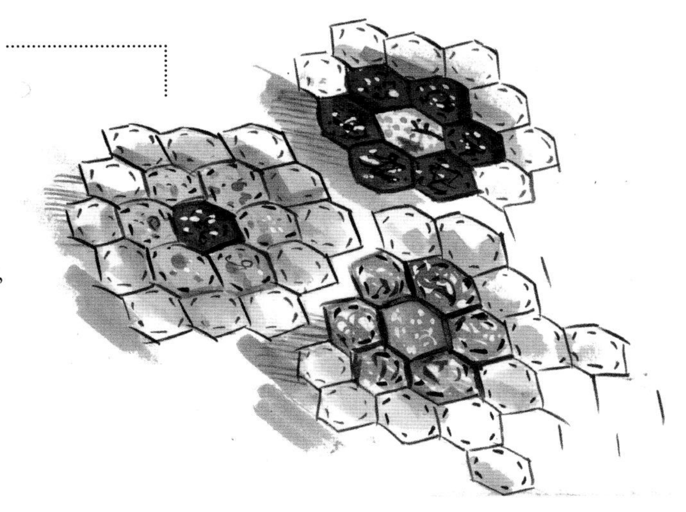

● THIS IS A PROJECT WHERE YOU WILL NEED TO USE TWO DIFFERENT TYPES OF SEWING NEEDLES: A MEDIUM LENGTH 'SHARP' FOR BASTING THE PATCHES TO THE TEMPLATES AND A FINE, SHORT 'BETWEEN' IN A SIZE 10 OR 11 FOR STITCHING THEM TOGETHER AND FOR HAND QUILTING.

Assembling the quilt When the day that you complete the patchwork eventually arrives, you can celebrate by unpicking the tacking stitches and removing all 373 backing papers. The finished quilt is made up of three layers. Spread out the first layer, which is the cotton backing, right side downwards and place the same-size wadding on top. Position the quilt top, right side upwards, centrally on the wadding. The layers need to be joined temporarily before they are sewn together. You can do this by working a 15cm grid of tacking stitches across the surface of the quilt, or by the quicker technique of simply pinning them together with small safety pins at regular intervals.

Trimming the wadding Whichever method you use, finish off by sewing or pinning the layers together around the outside edge. Carefully trim back the wadding so that the edge follows the shape of the quilt top and is in line with folded edges of the hexagons.

Sewing the edges together Cut away the surplus backing fabric, following the zigzag edge of the quilt top, but leaving a 1cm margin all around for the seam allowance. Make a small cut into the backing seam allowance at each inwards 'V'. Tack the backing to the quilt top as shown, turning the seam allowance inwards as you go, so the two match precisely. Overcast stitch the edges together all the way around the outside.

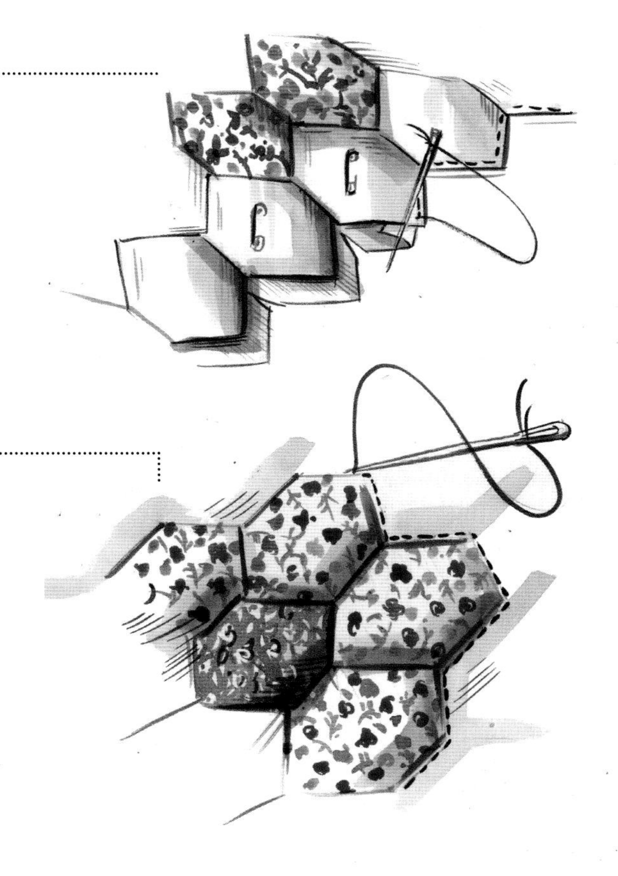

Working the quilting stitches Finally, stitch the three layers together, to give texture and depth to the quilt. Using a strong white quilting thread, work a line of small straight stitches around the outline of each rosette, sewing along the seam between the hexagons, or as quilters call it 'in the ditch. Remove all the safety pins and any remaining tacking.

● TAKE A TIP FROM VICTORIAN STITCHERS AND DRAW YOUR THREAD AGAINST A BLOCK OF SWEET-SMELLING BEESWAX. THIS HELPS IT TO GLIDE SMOOTHLY THROUGH THE PATCHES AS YOU SEW AND PREVENTS IT FROM FRAYING.

Contemporary Brick Quilt

This luxurious quilt is made up of seven different Liberty Tana Lawns carefully selected from a restricted palette of blues, browns and greys. Stitched together in rectangular patches, the separate prints appear less defined and the colours blend to create a painterly, muted effect. If you prefer something more dramatic, select bolder designs that are more varied in scale and hue. The patchwork is machine stitched, so very quick to put together, and the staggered brick layout means that there are no fussy matching of seams.

Finished quilt size

168cm wide by 220cm long, to fit a standard single bed (see Altering Quilt Size)

Brick patch size

Each full brick patch is cut 10 x 18cm; each finished brick measures 8.8 x 16.8cm

You will need

- For quilt top, 60cm of 136cm wide Liberty Tana Lawn in each of 'Capel', 'Carolyn Jane', 'Christhl', 'Dorothy Watton', 'Mauvey', 'Poppy & Daisy' and 'Wiltshire', a lightweight cotton fabric in seven different small-scale prints in harmonising shades
- For quilt backing, 4.2m of a 112cm wide solid-coloured lightweight cotton fabric
- For quilt binding, 80cm of a 112cm wide lightweight cotton fabric in another solid colour
- Lightweight cotton or bamboo quilt wadding, 180 x 232cm
- Matching sewing thread
- Quilting thread, in a toning grey
- Rotary cutter and mat, and quilter's ruler
- Safety pins (can be ordinary ones, but quilter's ones are good with a little bend in them)

Altering quilt size

The instructions are for a quilt for a standard single bed. To make a wider quilt, add more bricks across each horizontal row; to make a longer quilt, add to the number of horizontal rows. Follow the instructions for the single-bed quilt, keeping these changes in mind. For example, for a double-bed-size quilt, increase the width to 12½ bricks to achieve a 210cm wide quilt, and keep the length the same (25 rows of bricks). You will also need to increase the fabric amounts – for a double-bed-size quilt, you will need 70cm of each of seven different Tana Lawn fabrics; 5.1m of backing fabric; 90cm of binding fabric; and a piece of wadding 222 x 232cm.

Cutting out

FROM EACH OF THE EIGHT QUILT TOP PRINTS:

- Cut six selvedge-to-selvedge strips, each 10cm wide. Cut seven 18cm long patches from five of these strips, and four from the sixth strip, for a total of 39 brick patches (in each fabric). Save the ends of all the selvedge-to-selvedge strips to use at the quilt edges to stagger the positions of the bricks in the rows.

FROM BACKING FABRIC:

- Cut the backing fabric to the same size as wadding.

FROM BINDING FABRIC:

- Using a rotary cutter and cutting mat, cut eight selvedge-to-selvedge strips, each 9cm wide.

Arranging the patches The fabrics are arranged fairly randomly, but avoid placing identical patches next to each other. Lay out each row in turn to ensure you have a good balance of colour and pattern. Lay out the top horizontal row of bricks, using 10 brick patches positioned end-to-end. (The quilt is exactly 10 brick patches wide.) Arrange the next 7 horizontal rows below this, using 11 brick patches in each of these rows, so you can shift the position of the short vertical seams between the patches (the excess will be cut off later). Use the partial brick patches at the beginning of some rows if desired, but make sure each 11-brick row is long enough to cover the 10-brick width plus at least 2.5cm extra. Continue in this way, using 10 full patches across every eighth row and 11 patches across the remaining rows so you can shift the vertical seam positions, until there are 25 rows. Every other row will start at the right with a long patch and every other row with a short patch. Once your arrangement is finalised, you are ready to start stitching patches together.

Stitching together the first row of patches Stitch the first horizontal row of 10 patches together first. Pin the short ends of the first two patches together, with right sides together, and machine stitch 6mm from the edge. Stitch the next 8 patches to the first two in the same way. Press all the seam allowances in the same direction, towards the left.

Stitching together the patches in the remaining rows Stitch the remaining rows together in the same way, pressing seams to the left. Lay the rows out again in their correct positions, with the vertical seam allowances misaligned to create the brick effect. Trim the rows to the same length, or a little longer than the 10-patch rows. Remember every other row starts at the right with a long patch (of varying lengths – 10–18cm) and every other row with a short patch (of varying lengths – 5–9cm). Align the right-hand edge of the quilt rows as much as possible as this is the end from which you will be stitching the rows together.

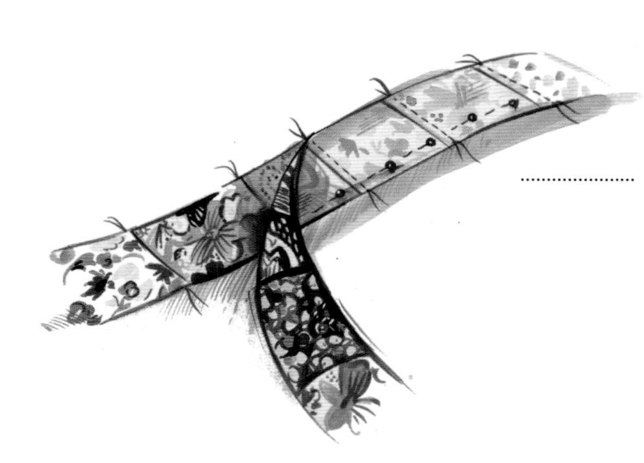

Stitching the horizontal rows together Pin the top edge of the second row to the bottom edge of the first row, with right sides together. Machine stitch with a 6mm seam allowance. Stitch from the right corner, so all the short seams are facing away from the presser foot as you stitch. Press the long seam downwards. Stitch on all the remaining rows in the same way.

Squaring off the edges Using a long ruler, draw a straight line along each side edge, and trim any overlapping patches.

Assembling the quilt The three layers of a quilt are traditionally basted with long lines of hand stitches, but using safety pins to temporarily join the quilt top, wadding and backing is a quicker new alternative. Unwrap the wadding and lay it out flat on the (clean!) floor, smoothing out any wrinkles and creases. Lay the patchwork top centrally on top, with the excess wadding sticking out roughly the same amount all around the edge of the top. Starting at the bottom edge, pin each rectangle to the wadding. A quilter's ruler will help you keep the seam lines parallel. Keep on smoothing the layers as you go.

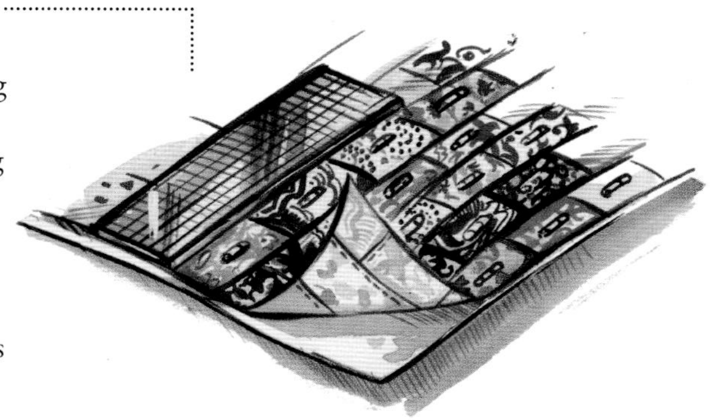

Adding the backing Turn the patchwork and wadding the other way up and spread the backing over them, aligning the edges of the backing with the edges of the wadding. Safety pin the backing to the other two layers, again ensuring that there are no wrinkles in the cloth.

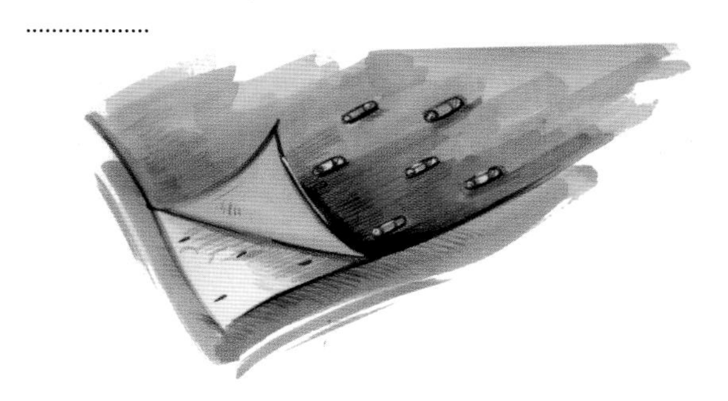

Working the quilting stitches The three layers are sewn together along the horizontal seam lines. Work long rows of quilting stitches in toning grey thread, either to one side of the seam or 'in the ditch' – directly over the join. You can do the quilting by hand or machine.

Beginning the binding When you finish the quilting, tack the three layers together close to the edge of the quilt top. Then trim the wadding and backing in line with the quilt top. Machine stitch the eight binding strips together end-to-end with a 6mm seam and press the seams open. From this long strip, cut two strips as long as the two long sides of the quilt. Press these binding strips in half lengthways with wrong sides together. Pin one of the strips to one long side of the right side of the quilt with the raw edges aligned. Machine stitch 1.5mm from the edge. Stitch the other strip to the other long side of the quilt in the same way.

Finishing the binding Turn the two side bindings to the wrong side and slipstitch the fold to the back of the quilt. Next, cut two bindings each 5cm longer than the quilt top and bottom. Stitch one to the top edge of the quilt and one to the bottom edge as for the first two binding, but leaving a 2.5cm excess at each end. Fold these bindings over to the wrong side of the quilt, folding in the excess at each end over the raw edges of the side bindings. Slipstitch the folded ends together, then stitch the long edge to the quilt back.

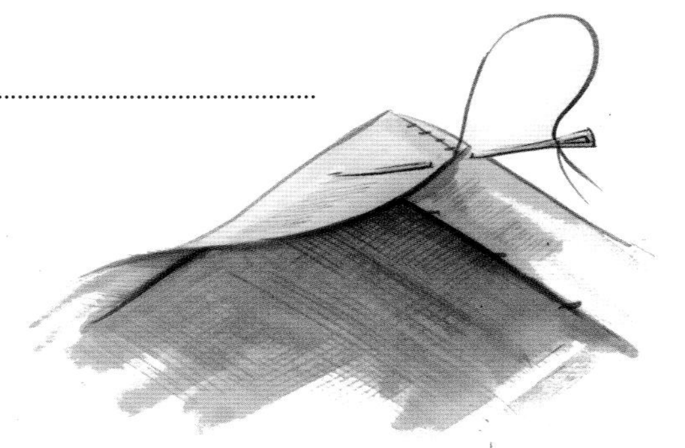

● A FLAT COTTON SHEET MAKES AN IDEAL BACKING FOR A QUILT. THEY COME IN SIZES UP TO 280CM SQUARE FOR A SUPERKING, SO THERE WILL BE NO NEED FOR SEAMING WHATEVER THE DIMENSIONS OF YOUR FINISHED PATCHWORK.

Sewing Basics

Essential Equipment

Sewing shops and online craft stores are packed with all kinds of fascinating gadgets, but when it comes to stocking up your work box, remember that you will only need a few basic items to make any of the projects in this book. It's always worth investing in the best quality tools however; they will last a long time and help you achieve a professional result.

Scissors

You'll need three pairs of scissors, in three different sizes and each with its own purpose.

- LARGE TAILOR'S SHEARS with long blades are important for accurate cutting. They have an angled handle that keeps the lower blade flat against the table as you cut. Buy a good quality steel shears that can be sharpened when necessary and look out for a pair with comfortable cushioned handles. Remember not to use these for paper as this tends to blunt the blades.
- MEDIUM HOUSEHOLD SCISSORS can be used for cutting out smaller items and all of your patterns and templates.
- SMALL EMBROIDERY SCISSORS with a sharp point are ideal for snipping threads, notching seams and clipping corners.

Rotary cutting

A round-bladed rotary cutter looks like a pastry wheel. It is always used alongside a perspex quilter's ruler, marked with a regular grid, and a self-healing plastic mat. These tools are designed for patchwork, but are a very quick and efficient way of making squares and rectangles to given measurements. The largest-sized mat and a 60cm ruler will speed up your general fabric cutting, but watch your fingers. Those blades are very sharp, so cut away from you at all times!

Needles

There are different types of needle for various hand sewing tasks, so start off with an assorted packet. They come in various thicknesses: the higher the number the more slender the needle; you'll soon discover what feels comfortable to work with. Store them in a felt-leaved needle book, a needle case or keep them in the packet – they disappear into pincushions.

- SHARPS are the most useful for everyday hand stitching and tacking. They are medium length and have a small eye to accommodate a single strand of sewing thread.
- BETWEENS or QUILTING needles are shorter and finer, and will easily go through several layers of fabric.
- CREWEL needles have longer eyes for stranded embroidery cotton and as these are easy to thread, can also be used for general sewing.

Pins

Steel dressmaker's pins and brass lace pins are fine, about 2.5cm long and have tiny heads. Both are good for pinning Liberty Tana Lawn as they leave no marks but longer glass-headed pins are easier to use and show up against patterned fabrics. Store your pins in a tin (with a small magnet) or a homemade pincushion, like the extravagant Peacock Pincushion on pages 76–81.

Safety pins

Standard safety pins are always handy and can be used for threading ribbon or cord through casings. Special quilter's safety pins are an invaluable alternative to traditional tacking techniques when assembling a quilt – they have a bend in them like old-fashioned nappy pins so they can easily slip in and out of the layers.

Measuring up

A good long tape measure is vital and spring-loaded retractable ones are the tidiest. Special geometric sewing gauges are marked with common measurements checking the depth of hems and turnings, but a simple 15cm ruler does the same job.

Marking tools

Dressmaker's felt pens are a great innovation: they have a light-sensitive pigment that fades in time, and can be used to draw seam allowances or embroidery outlines. Tailor's chalk shows up on darker and thicker fabrics, and a sharp HB pencil provides a light outline on fine cloth. If you want a guide mark that leaves no trace, copy the old Welsh quilters by running the tip of a needle against a ruler and stitching along the score line.

Iron

You will need to iron your fabric before cutting out and to press the seams as you work, so keep a steam iron and large ironing board to hand. A diffuser spray is helpful for stubborn creases whilst fabric stiffener can help when cutting out small shapes from fine fabrics.

Useful bits and bobs

- A THIMBLE gives vital protection for quilting (when you may need one on each hand) and for large amounts of hand stitching. If you haven't used one before, they can feel clumsy and ungainly, but do persevere. Antique silver has its own charm, but steel is more practical and new flexible silicone thimbles are best of all, moulding to fit your finger tip.
- A BLOCK OF BEESWAX is useful for patchwork projects. Draw a length of thread against it to give a fine wax coating to help your stitches glide through the fabric and prevent fraying.
- A LINT ROLLER keeps your work and workspace tidy by gathering up all the snipped threads and the tiniest fragments of fabric.

Haberdashery

In addition to all this equipment, there is a vast array of fabulous haberdashery or notions: the threads, braids, buttons, satin ribbons and sequins used to create and embellish your stitchery. All true stitchers will collect these, magpie-like, and store them for future projects and it's always good to have a varied hoard to choose from.

Sewing threads

Keep a large spool of white poly-cotton sewing thread in your work box, along with black and a few other basic colours. When buying for a particular project, you should match the thread to the fabric as closely as possible. If you can't find an exact match, or if there isn't a single dominant colour in the pattern, go for a slightly darker shade. Match fibre to fibre when choosing your thread: finely spun mercerised cotton thread is best for sewing Liberty Tana Lawn, and poly-cotton works well with canvas and slightly stretchy needlecord. Thicker, stronger quilting thread comes many shades and is used for, of course, hand quilting.

Buttons & beads

Buttons aren't just for fastening your clothes. One-off single buttons make striking focal points, so buy them when you see them, or rummage through your friends' and family's button jars in search of hidden treasures. I used a lustrous pearl coat button in the centre of the Round Cushion on pages 88–91 whilst a black and white vintage plastic button was the perfect finishing touch on the Frilly Pinny with Potholder on pages 106–11. Used with restraint, glass beads add light and colour: those on the Jewellery Roll on pages 64–7 are 'worry' beads from a shop in Athens.

Fabric-covered buttons add a sophisticated look to cushions and bench seats and come in easy-to-use kits, from 8–50mm in diameter. All you have to do is cut a circle of fabric and gather it round a domed top part, then press on the backing and shank. Liberty Tana Lawn is perfect for covering buttons as the prints are so finely detailed: look for interesting motifs and centre them within the circle.

Press studs

Also known as poppers or snap fasteners, these miniature feats of engineering are a nineteenth-century invention, favoured by designers of Western shirts and children's garments alike for their practicality. The detachable cloth on the Cook's Apron on pages 30–35 is fixed with on press studs, and the Tote Bag on pages 52–7 converts to a neat handbag by folding in the corners and snapping them together.

Zips

Traditional sofa cushion covers have piping around the edge and are fastened with a zip, but I've gone for a softer, less structured look for the Basic Cushions on pages 14–19 and Bench Cushion on pages 102–05. However, inserting a zip means that covers can easily be removed for laundering, and it wouldn't be a difficult task to add a zip to the long side gusset of the Bench Cushion.

Zips come in a range of colours and weights, metal zips being heavier and tougher than nylon versions. If you can't find the right length, pick one longer than you need and trim the end to size. I customised the zips in the Washbag on pages 40–43 by adding a decorative leather pull to the slider.

Fusible adhesive bonding web

This twentieth-century innovation is a heat-sensitive adhesive mounted on paper. It melts with the heat of an iron to bond two layers of fabric together and comes in heavy- and light-bond weights. Choose a heavy bond for thicker fabrics and light-bond for Liberty Tana Lawn. I used bonding web to appliqué the luscious roses on the Rose Throw on pages 122–27 and to make a two-sided fabric for the petals of the Rose Corsage on pages 92–5.

Getting Started

Making the patterns

Many of the projects – including the Round Cushion on pages 88–91 and Jewellery Roll on pages 64–7 – are made from simple squares and rectangles. The dimensions for these are given with the instructions. To make the paper patterns you can simply transfer the measurements for the width and depth to dressmaker's squared pattern paper (like giant sheets of graph paper printed with a grid) and cut out along the printed lines.

A few more complicated projects, like the Frilly Pinny with Potholder on pages 106–11 and the Kimono on pages 112–17, involve curved lines. These templates are given in a scaled-down version on a square grid on which each square is the equivalent to a specified dimension. Draw them up to scale by copying the outline, square for square, onto dressmaker's pattern paper. Small templates like the Rose Corsage petals on page 92 and the Peacock Pincushion pieces on page 78 are shown at 50% of their full size and so can be photocopied at 200% to give the correct size template.

The size and shape of other, more individual, makes is variable and will depend on the size of your window, bench, cushion or notice board. Guidance is given for measuring up and working out the proportions for these projects. Before you cut out, always double check that your pattern is the correct size.

Working with fabric

Look closely at the fabric and you'll see that it's made up of two sets of interwoven threads at right angles to each other. The long threads that are set on to the loom are called the warp and run from top to bottom. The threads that are woven between them are called the weft, and run from side to side. The woven edges are known as the selvedges. Always cut these off, as the fabric here is often more tightly woven.

Your pattern pieces should always be positioned so that the side edges are parallel to the selvedges, and they lie squarely on the 'long grain' of the fabric. Pieces that are not cut on the grain can stretch and become distorted.

If you pull the fabric from corner to corner you'll realise just how much 'give' there is in a plain weave. Fabric cut diagonally is said to be 'on the bias' or cross grain, and will hang or drape in a much more fluid way – a characteristic exploited by 1930s evening wear designers. Stretchy bias strips are used for making rouleaux and for binding curved edges, like those at the front of the Kimono.

Many of the Liberty Tana Lawns have small-scale overall patterns, so the actual position of the templates isn't critical, but on larger designs they should be placed symmetrically for a pleasingly balanced appearance. Allow extra fabric for this, particularly for a project like the paisley Basic Square Cushion, which was inspired by Liberty silk scarves. Centre large motifs and when cutting horizontal or vertical strips, pick an interesting part of the design.

Cutting out

Press your material to get rid of any creases or wrinkles before you pin on the patterns, then smooth it out flat on a large table or floor. Pin on the pattern pieces lining them up along the grain. Cut out around the outside edges with tailor's shears, keeping the angled blade down and making long strokes rather than 'nibbling' at the fabric. Alternatively you can cut out smaller rectangular pieces with a rotary cutter and clear quilter's ruler. This is a good method for bulk making patchwork pieces: fold and press the fabric and you can do several at a time.

Know your sewing machine

You may well be an experienced stitcher with a trusted sewing machine that you've been using for years, but the new enthusiast can be bewildered by the range of machines that are now available. These range from simple plastic entry-level machines to very expensive high-tech electronic models that can be linked to PCs to produce complex embroideries. Go to a reputable dealer or department store if you are buying a new sewing machine. Try them all out and spend time talking to the knowledgeable sales team, but don't be tempted to overspend. Study the manual carefully – it will tell you all you need to know about your particular model and will have a useful troubleshooting section.

All you need to make any of the projects in this book is a good solid machine with some basic functions: the ability to cope with thicker fabrics, a zigzag stitch for neatening seams and a regular straight stitch with even an tension. Most machines come with a selection of feet, some of which are very complicated. You'll probably use the transparent sewing foot most of the time, but the narrow zipper foot is necessary for sewing in zips.

Some machines will automatically adjust the presser foot when sewing different weight fabrics, but on others you have to change a lever. Don't forget to do this, as a fine fabric needs less pressure than a thick one. The only other thing you need to remember is to buy plenty of needles and to match the gauge of the needle to the material being sewn: fine for lawn and a thicker, denim weight for canvas. Change needles regularly, as a blunt or snagged point will cause the stitches to become irregular. Other routine maintenance involves brushing out cotton fluff from the bobbin case and occasionally applying a little oil as directed.

Hems and Edges

There are two ways to neaten the edge of a piece of fabric: by turning it back and stitching down the fold to make a hem or by binding it with a narrow strip of fabric. If you can hem a panel of fabric you can easily make your own window treatments: the Roman Blind or Simple Curtains both involve maximum visual impact and minimal sewing technique!

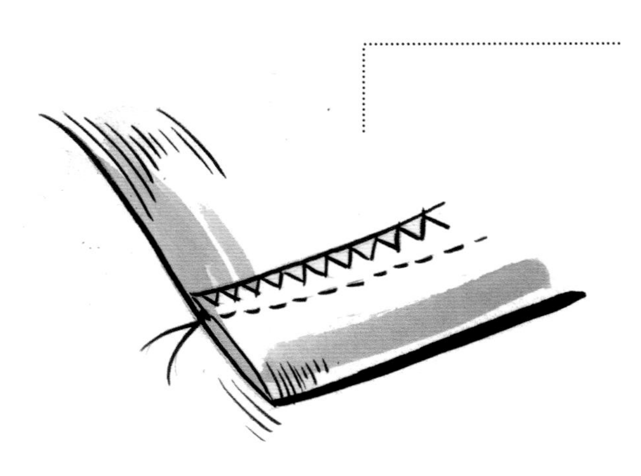

Single hem

Enclose the edges with an overlocking stitch or zigzag. With the right side facing downwards, fold back the neatened edge to the depth specified in the instructions from one corner to the other, pressing it with a hot iron as you go. Use a ruler to ensure that the turning is the same all the way along. Pin the turning down, then machine stitch just below the zigzag, or hem stitch by hand (see page 153) for a more discreet finish.

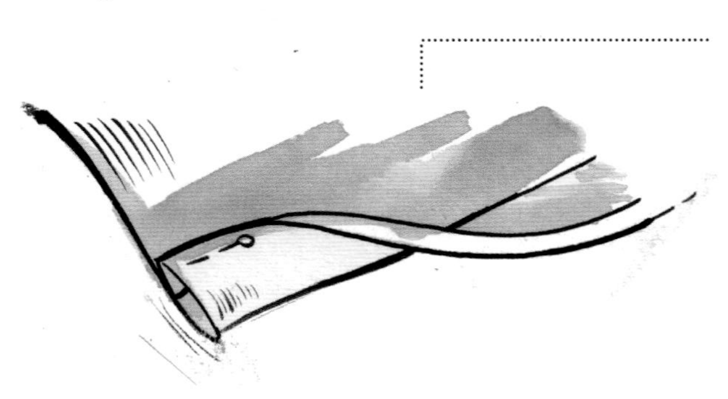

Double hem

This more durable finish consists of two turnings, the first one usually being shorter than the second. Fold and press the first turning as above, then measure and press a second turning so that the raw edge is concealed. Pin in place and sew the folded edge down by hand or machine.

Mitre

When two equal hems meet at a right angles, the surplus fabric is trimmed and neatly folded into an origami-like mitre to prevent the corner from becoming bulky. Unfold the two creases on each side and trim a triangle from the corner, cutting through the folded square. Refold the creases. Slip stitch the diagonals and sew down the folded edges.

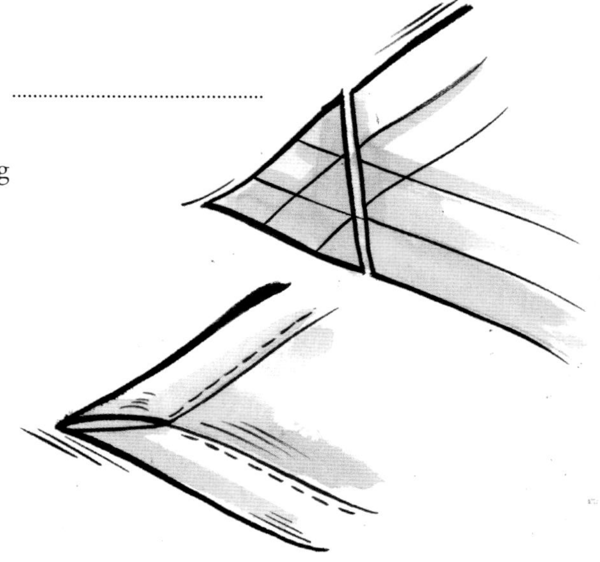

Bound edge

For a straight edge use ready-made bias binding or cut your own from a straight grain strip of fabric, four times the finished depth. Press the binding in half, then press the raw edges to the centre crease and unfold. Pin the binding along the edge of the fabric with right sides facing and machine stitch along the first crease line. Refold the bottom crease and turn the binding to the back. Slipstitch the fold or machine stitch just inside the edge of the binding. The Jewellery Roll is bound in this way. To bind a curved edge, like the inside seams on the Washbag, you must use a bias strip or bias binding.

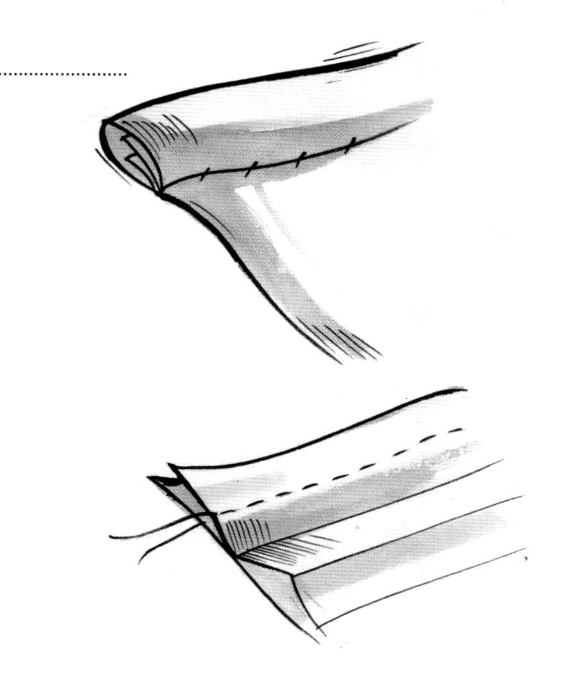

Seams

Before you stitch two pieces of fabric together you need to join them temporarily with pins and/or tacking. Hold them with right sides together and insert pins through both layers at each corner, then along the rest of the edge. You can either do this with the pins at right angles to the seam line, so that they can easily be removed as the fabric passes under the presser foot, or position them parallel to the edge. A line of tacking – long running stitches – makes a stable foundation for machine stitching. Sew just inside the seam line with a contrasting colour and remove the thread when the seam is complete.

The width of the seam allowance – the spare fabric that lies within a seam – is specified for each individual project; it's usually 1cm or 1.5cm wide, although patchwork is often joined with a narrow 6mm seam. To keep this width consistent, line the raw edges up along the corresponding engraved parallel line on the sewing machine base plate and hold them in this position as you stitch. Press each seam as it is completed to give your work a crisp finish.

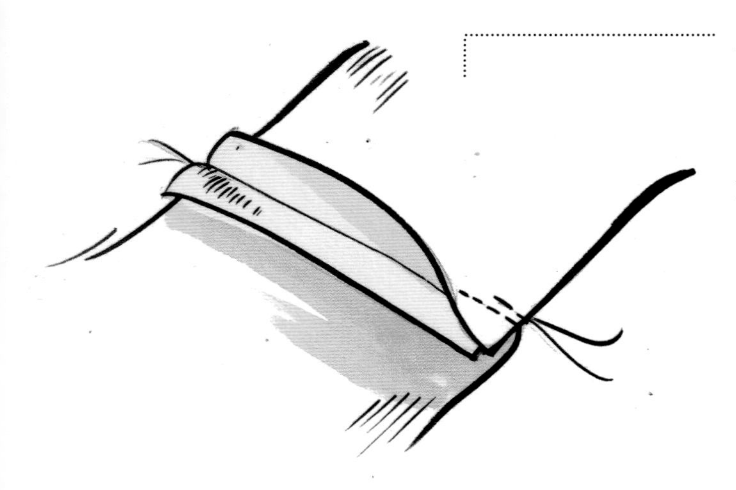

Straight seam

Sew the two edges together along the given seam allowance. Reinforce both ends of the seam line with a few backwards stitches so that it won't unravel – check your instruction manual to find the reverse lever. Press the seam allowance open or to one side as directed.

Topstitched seam

Topstitching reinforces a seam and gives a neat finish. Press the seam allowance to one side then sew through all three layers on the right side, 3mm from the seam line, using the inside space on presser foot as a guide.

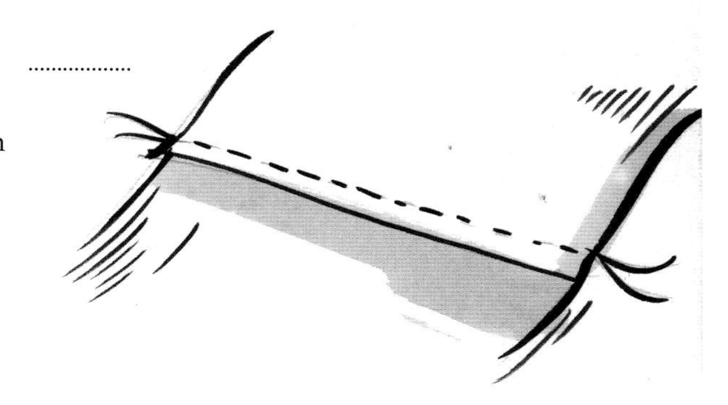

Corner seam

Stitch along the seam allowance as far as the corner. Keeping the needle down, lift the presser foot and pivot the fabric around through a right angle. Continue along the next edge. Trim away the surplus fabric at the corner in a triangle shape. Turn right side out and ease out the point with the tips of your embroidery scissors or a pencil.

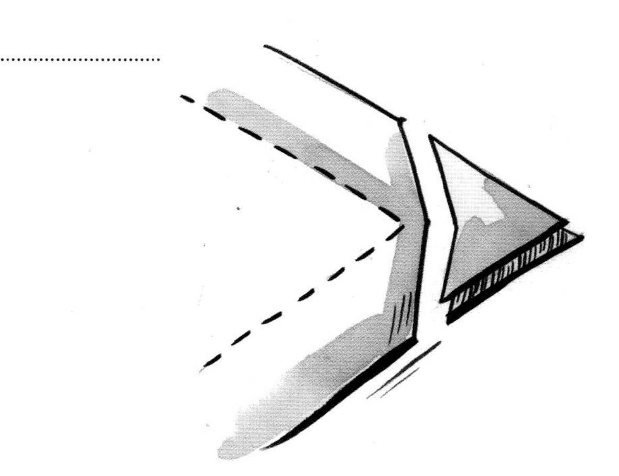

Curved seams

Trim the seam allowance down to 6mm to reduce the bulk. Around an outside curve you will need to cut out a series of tiny triangles to within 3mm of the stitch line and on an inside curve make a row of little snips into the seam allowance. This enables the seam to lie flat when it is turned right side out and pressed.

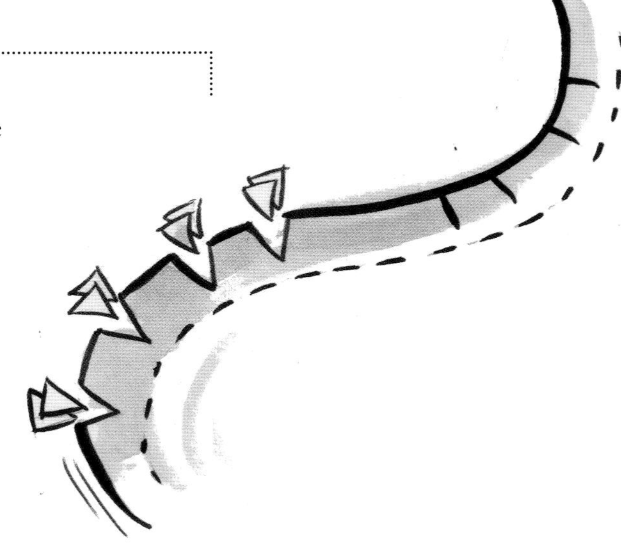

Hand Stitches

Careful preparation and hand finishing give a professional look to any needlework project, so here are the six simple stitches that you will need to gather, tack, finish seams and turn up hems.

Running stitch

This is the foundation of all hand stitches and so basic that it needs no explanation. Use it for gathering frills and for quilted outlines. The spaces and stitches are the same size and the length should be between 5–8mm long depending on the thickness of the cloth. With practice, and using a longer needle, you should be able to pick up two or three stitches at a time. Make longer stitches when tacking, or use the dressmaker's variation below.

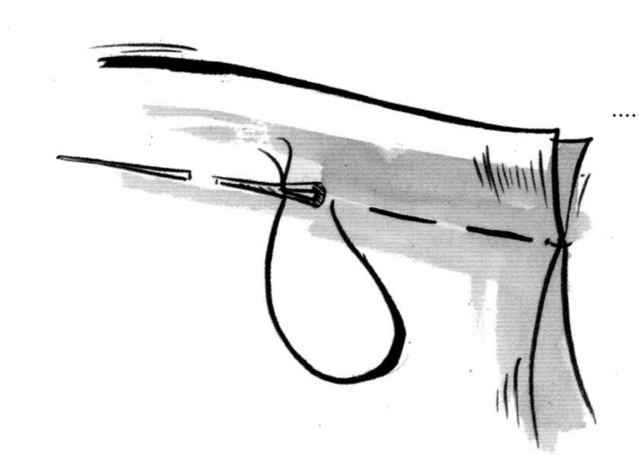

Tacking

A quickly worked temporary stitch, a line of tacking holds two pieces of fabric together before they are machine stitched. The length of the individual stitches doesn't really matter as long as the seam is aligned accurately, but generally they should be about 2cm long for canvas and thicker fabrics and 1cm for finer materials. The stitches are about twice as long as the spaces between them.

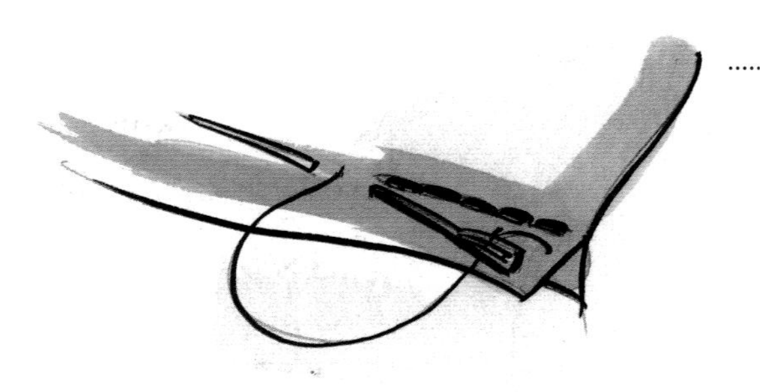

Backstitch

Use this for seaming the hand sewing where more strength is needed. Follow the seam line from right to left. Bring the needle out one stitch length ahead of the previous stitch and work each stitch backwards, from left to right. Keep all the stitches the same length.

Slipstitch

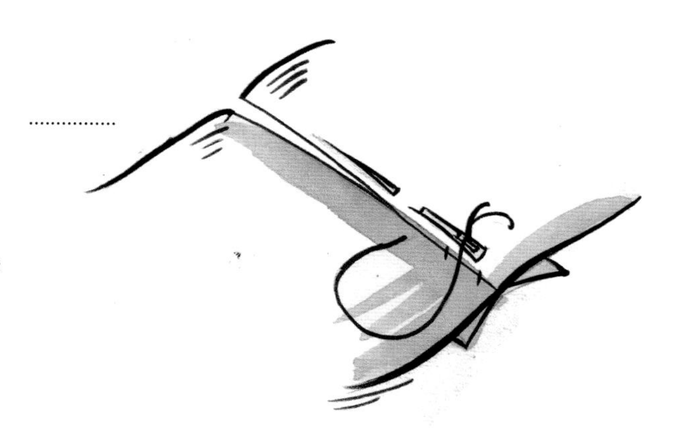

This joining stitch produces a flat, unobtrusive seam. It's used to hold together two folded edges at a mitred corner or on either side of an opening (like that on the Basic Cushions). Bring the needle out through the bottom fold and, keeping it roughly horizontal, insert the point directly above through the top fold. Push the tip through the top fold so that it emerges 5mm further along, then pull the needle through. Insert it directly below and repeat the same action to the end of the space.

Slip hemming

Favoured by dressmakers because it is barely visible on the right side of the fabric, this stitch is useful for hemming blinds and curtains. Only the smallest amount – a single thread on canvas – of the main fabric is taken up by the needle. Bring the needle up through the folded hem and pick up a tiny stitch of fabric with the tip. Pull through and take the needle back into the hem directly below the stitch. Keeping it horizontal, push the point up 5mm further along and continue stitching to the end of the hem. Try not to pull the thread too hard or make the stitches tight or the fabric will pucker.

Stab stitch

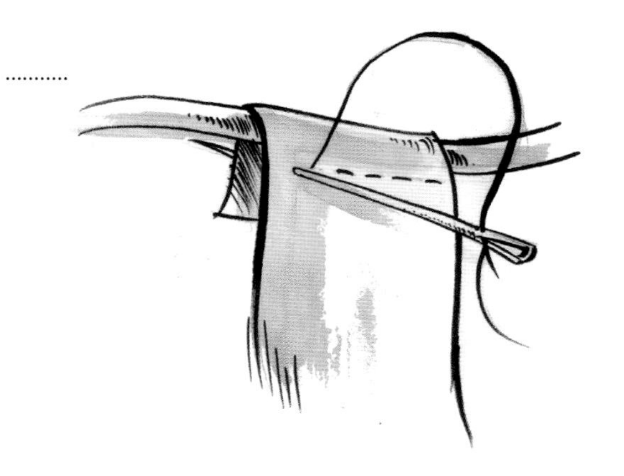

As its name suggests, you make an up and down stabbing action with the needle for this stitch, rather than the usual smooth horizontal glide. It produces small, strong stitches which secure two or more layers of fabric together, often in awkward areas: I used it to attach the fabric strips to the lampshade frame on page 118. Starting from the back, bring the needle up through all the layers, then take it vertically down, about 3mm away, in the direction along the seam. Bring it back up in the same way to continue.

Appliqué Translating from French as 'put on', this is a decorative textile technique in which cut-out fabric shapes are sewn onto a background to create a new design.

Backstitch Used for hand seaming, these small regular stitches are made from right to left.

Batten A strip of wood with a square or rectangular section, used for mounting a blind onto a wall or window frame.

Bias binding This ready-made trim consists of a continuous bias strip of cotton or satinised fabric with pressed back edges. It is used for binding straight and curved edges and comes in a wide range of colours and several widths. Special gadgets are available to create neat turnings if you want to make binding from your own fabric.

Bias grain The bias grain lies diagonally across the intersection of the straight and cross grains of a woven fabric and can be found by drawing a line at 45 degrees to the selvedge. A fabric strip or angled edge cut 'on the bias' will have a lot of stretch, or give.

Blind acorn A hollow metal or wooden connector, in the form of an acorn, through which the ends of the lifting cords on a Roman blind are threaded. The unusual shape derives from an ancient belief that the oak tree provides protection from lightning.

Blind ring Made from metal or plastic these tiny (1cm) rings are sewn to the back of Roman or festoon blinds in vertical rows. The lifting cords are threaded through the rings so that the blind can be drawn up.

Box cushion As the name suggests, this a square or rectangular, box-shaped cushion made to fit a bench or recessed window seat. It's padded with safety-grade upholstery foam, which can be ordered to size from local or online suppliers.

Buttonhole thread Sometimes known as 'buttonhole twist', this is a thick, tightly spun thread used by tailors for hand-stitched buttonholes. It is very strong and so can be used for many other sewing tasks.

Calico This is an unbleached straight weave cotton fabric that comes in several weights, and is useful for backings and linings.

Cleat A nautical term, a cleat is a metal fitting that is screwed close to a window frame. It has two projections around which the lifting cords are wound when a blind is drawn up.

Corsage Now used to describe a real or faux flower worn on the lapel, wrist or waist, a corsage was originally the name for a fitted dress bodice.

Cushion pad Cotton-covered ready-made pads are available in a wide range of shapes and sizes, with duck feather or polyester fibre fillings. Check that they meet current safety standards and are fire-resistant.

Cutting mat A self-healing cutting mat should always be used alongside a rotary cutter. The plastic surface has a non-slip finish that prevents the blade from blunting and is printed with a helpful grid. It's worth buying the largest size of mat to speed up your work.

D-ring Metal rings, in the shape of a capital letter 'D', are used for attaching straps and to make adjustable apron neck ties. You'll find them in a silver or gilt finish at hardware shops or sewing suppliers.

Double-face ribbon This is a reversible satin ribbon which has two smooth and shiny sides. Single-face ribbon is shiny on one side only.

Double-sided tape An item of stationery that should be in every work basket, this plastic tape has adhesive on both sides, and has many uses when sewing. It comes in 12mm–3cm widths.

Drawstring channel Also called a gathering channel, this is the space between two parallel lines of stitching at the opening of a bag, through which a cord or tape is threaded.

Dressmaker's pattern paper These large sheets of paper are printed with a square grid and are used for drawing full-size pattern pieces from scaled-down diagrams, or for cutting out shapes to given measurements.

Dressmaker's pins Choose between slender metal pins with tiny heads, or longer, thicker versions with bead-like round heads, depending on the fabric you are using. Keep them in a saucer for quick pinning when working, but replace them in a pincushion or secure tin afterwards.

Drill A mid- to heavy-weight cotton fabric with a diagonal weave, hardwearing drill is used for aprons and bags.

Drop The drop of a curtain or blind is the distance between the top and bottom edges. It will vary depending on the type of heading used and whether the curtain is to be sill, below sill or floor length.

Facing This is a piece of fabric used to neaten a raw edge, such as the front of a garment or the opening of a bag. It is often in a contrasting or different weight fabric.

Fusible adhesive bonding web A thin layer of heat-sensitive adhesive with a paper backing used to adhere two layers of fabric. It comes in both heavy and light bonds: choose the weight to match the fabric being used and follow the manufacturer's instructions carefully.

Gathering thread A line or circle of running stitches which is pulled up to create a frilled edge or line of gathers.

Grain Woven fabrics are made from two sets of threads at right angles to each other: the warp which is set onto the loom and runs from top to bottom (the long grain), and the weft, carried by the shuttle, which runs from left to right. Fabric pieces should always be cut along the grain of the fabric (i.e., with the side edges parallel to the long grain).

Green baize A durable cloth made from a mixture of wool and cotton, baize has a slightly rough surface. It's traditionally used to cover gaming tables, for snooker and cards, as well as office notice boards.

Gusset This is a strip of fabric used to give depth to a box cushion or to a bag.

Header This is the top edge of a curtain, from which it hangs. Fabric loops or ties can be stitched directly onto the header, or it may be finished with a specially woven curtain tape with drawstrings and slots for hooks.

Interfacing Available in iron-on or sew-in versions and several different weights, this is a non-woven material used to give extra strength and body to fabrics.

Lath A narrow strip of wood used to weight the bottom edge of a Roman blind so that it hangs correctly.

Lengthways As in 'fold in half lengthways': make a fold parallel to the longer edge of a piece of fabric.

Linen Woven from flax, linen is a hardwearing, long-lasting natural fabric, which improves with use. Use new or undamaged vintage linen for aprons or tea towels.

Mitre A mitred corner, where the seam allowance is folded at 45 degrees and trimmed, eliminates bulk and gives a very crisp finish: see how to do this on page 149.

Needlecord This is a fine corduroy fabric with very narrow ridges or ribs, which give it a fine textured surface. It's long been a favourite for making children's clothes but has many other uses.

Overlock Most domestic sewing machines have a functional overlocking stitch to use instead of a zigzag, but serious dressmakers invest in an overlocking machine which uses three or four threads and has a blade to trim seams as it stitches.

Patchwork A fabric made up by stitching together regularly shaped small pieces of material to create a pattern.

Pattern repeat The design on a printed fabric recurs at regular intervals along its length. Match up this pattern repeat when making matching sets, or on the front, back and sides of an item, to give a professional finish.

Polystyrene beads Buy safety standard polystyrene beads by volume for beanbags and vacuum up all the strays once your cover is filled.

Press 'Set' each seam as you finish it with a hot, dry iron. When pressing use an up-and-down rather than a gliding motion, which can distort the seam.

Quilter's ruler These clear perspex cutting guides come in several sizes and are printed with a grid for accurate measuring. Glue small strips of sandpaper to the reverse to prevent them from slipping.

Quilting thread A strong, tightly spun thread used for quilting outlines. Choose a colour to match or contrast with your background fabrics depending on whether or not you want the quilting stitches to be visible.

Rosette A term used in patchwork to describe a flower-like arrangement of seven hexagons. Increase the size of a rosette by adding further rounds in different fabrics.

Rotary cutter A sharp, round blade mounted on a handle, which is used for speedy cutting of fabric. For safety, choose one with a retractable blade, always cut away from you and use with a self-healing mat.

Rouleau A narrow roll or tube of fabric used to make fastening loops and ties. A rouleau turner is a useful but not essential tool.

Screw eye Small (2cm long) metal screws with a loop at the head, through which shade cords are threaded.

Seam The straight or curved line along which two pieces of fabric are stitched together.

Seam allowance The distance between the cut edge of the fabric and the seam line. This width varies, but is always specified in the instructions for each project.

Selvedge This is the name given to the two woven edges of a fabric. Don't be tempted to use the selvedge as a ready-made hem, as the tension here is tighter than in the centre. The long grain lies parallel to the selvedges.

Sewing thread Choose between cotton polyester, or all-purpose mixed fibres to match your fabric and be sure to by a large enough spool to finish the project.

Shears Long-bladed scissors used for cutting out fabric.

Slipstitch A hand sewing technique used for closing seams once an item has been turned through or for sewing a folded edge to the main fabric.

Staple gun This powered upholsterers' tool, used for inserting metal staples into wood, is helpful when stretching fabric over chair seats or boards.

Tacking Use a contrasting thread when working long tacking or basting stitches so that you can unpick them easily. Always tack a little distance from the seam line so that the threads are not caught under the machine stitches.

Tailor's chalk Moulded blocks of fine chalk used for drawing lines on fabric. White chalk is used for marking dark fabrics and red or blue for marking light cloth.

Tana Lawn Synonymous with Liberty, this 100% cotton fabric has a very fine thread count and soft, silky feel. New print designs are created each season, heritage classics are continuously reworked and there is also an array of co-ordinating plain colors.

Tapestry needle Very large-eyed, blunt-ended needles are used for needlepoint embroidery but are helpful for threading ribbon.

Template A pattern piece which may be given actual size or scaled down. Templates are given for many of the projects in this book.

Topstitch A reinforcing line of machine stitch, worked close to a finished seam.

Toy filling Soft-textured, safety grade polyester filling with a long staple or fibre length, should always be used for toys, and is also useful for making non-allergenic cushion pads.

Turn right side out Turn a finished item through an opening left in one of the seams. Ease the seams by rolling them between your fingers so that they lie at the edge, then push the corners out into points with a blunt pencil (or a dressmaker's turning tool from a sewing supplier).

Upholstery nail Used for fastening fabric to seat frames, these metal pins have domed heads, sometimes embossed, and long shafts. Protect the head with a layer of cloth when hammering them into place.

Wadding Also called batting, this soft fibre is used to pad quilts. Choose between natural (cotton, bamboo or silk), synthetic (polyester, microfibre or recycled) or blended fibres.

Widthways As in 'fold in half widthways': make the fold parallel to the shorter edges of the fabric.

Zigzag A sewing-needle machine stitch used to neaten raw edges when seaming. Test first on a fabric offcut to find the best length and distance between the stitches.

Zipper foot A narrow sewing machine foot used when stitching zips. Always remember to change the needle position when the zipper foot is in place.

Amelia Star was designed for the autumn/winter 2011 season. The design of waves of mixed flowers was inspired by 1970s glam rock music.
TANA LAWN *Used on the Washbag (pages 40–43)*

Bailando En Mis Suenos was designed for the autumn/winter 2011 season. This is the first season Liberty has produced a group of digital prints. This chalk pastel drawn hibiscus flower was inspired by Cuban music.
BALCOMBE SILK *Used on the Kimono (pages 112–17)*

Betsy is a stylised small floral, created for Liberty in 1933 by an unknown designer with the initials 'DS'. It has been on Classic Tana Lawn since 1982.
TANA LAWN *Used on the Cook's Apron (pages 30–35)*

Caesar is a print that takes a fresh look at the peacock feather, symbol of the Aesthetic Movement, which has always been associated with Liberty.
TANA LAWN *Used on the Peacock Pincushion (pages 76–81)*

Capel is a one-colour floral that was first printed on Tana Lawn in 1978. Capel has been in the Classic Tana Lawn collection since 1993.
TANA LAWN *Used on the Gadget Case (pages 72–75), Traditional Cot Quilt (pages 128–33) and Contemporary Brick Quilt (pages 134–39)*

Carline is based on 1950s-style roses. It was designed for Liberty in 1994 and has been on Classic Tana Lawn since 1997.
TANA LAWN *Used on the Frilly Pinny with Potholder (page 106–11)*

Carolyn Jane was designed for the spring/summer 2011 season. The line drawn poppies were inspired by a 1920s pattern book in the Liberty archive.
TANA LAWN *Used on the Contemporary Brick Quilt (pages 134–39)*

Christhl was designed for the spring/summer 2011 season. It is part of a group of finely-drawn paisley designs.
TANA LAWN *Used on the Contemporary Brick Quilt (pages 134–39)*

Combe is based on a nineteenth-century textile in the Liberty archive. It was designed for silk in the autumn/winter 2011 season.
HARCOURT SILK CREPE DE CHINE *Used on the Kimono (pages 112–17)*

David Joe is an ethereal design inspired by gardens from Indian miniatures. Created by picture book author and illustrator, Jane Ray, it features hand-painted watercolour trees.
TANA LAWN *Used on the Round Cushion (pages 88–91)*

Dorothy Watton was designed for the spring/summer 2011 season. It was inspired by details in the Liberty shop and has a distinct Arts & Crafts feel to it.
TANA LAWN *Used on the Contemporary Brick Quilt (pages 134–39)*

Douglas Stripe is based on colourway strips of a 1970s Liberty design. It was designed for the spring/summer 2011 season.
TANA LAWN *Used on the Traditional Cot Quilt (pages 128–33)*

Edenham has been on Classic Tana Lawn since 1997. This design was originally bought in for the spring/summer 1994 season.
TANA LAWN *Used on the Round Cushion – Taking It Further (page 91)*

Eleanabella was designed for the autumn/winter 2011 season. It is based on the decade of the noughties with a pattern that is made up of different floral textures laid layer upon layer.
TANA LAWN *Used on the Jewellery Roll (pages 64–67)*

Eloise is a dense all-over floral design from the mid-1950s. It is based on a mixture of a late-nineteenth-century swatches in Liberty's pattern books.
TANA LAWN *Used on the Traditional Cot Quilt (pages 128–33)*

Elysian is from the Liberty archive. It was used by both dress and furnishing fabrics on a lightweight cotton in the late 1910s, early 1920s. It has been on Classic Tana Lawn since 1979.
TANA LAWN *Used on the Keepsake Board (pages 60–63)*

Explosions in the Sky was designed for the autumn/winter 2011 season. It is inspired by the music of a 1960s instrumental band and a Jimi Hendrix poster.
TANA LAWN *Used on the Lampshade (pages 118–21)*

Fairford is a floral print that represents the essence of Liberty style. The design was taken from the archive and painstakingly re-drawn to create a new Classic Tana Lawn.
TANA LAWN *Used on the Traditional Cot Quilt (pages 128–33)*

Glenjade is a pattern originally from a 1930s Liberty cotton design by an unknown designer. It has been on Classic Tana Lawn since 1997.
TANA LAWN *Used on the Frilly Pinny with Potholder (pages 106–111)*

Helena's Party was designed for the spring/summer 2011 season. It is based on a design in the archive of 1937.
TANA LAWN *Used on the Book Covers (pages 82–85)*

Kate Ada was designed for the spring/summer 2011 season.
The line drawn roses were inspired by a 1920s pattern book in the Liberty archive.
TANA LAWN *Used on the Rose Throw (pages 122–27)*

Kate Nouveau is based on a block-printed design in the archive. Liberty produced it in the early 1900s and it was part of the Art Nouveau revival in the 1960s. It has returned to the range for autumn/winter 2012.
COTTON CANVAS *Used on the Roman Blind (pages 44–47)*

Kayoko was designed for the spring/summer 2011 season. The dense small flowers were inspired by a design in a 1920s pattern book in the Liberty archive.
TANA LAWN *Used on the Eco Shopper (pages 24–29)*

Lodden is an original William Morris design, first produced by Morris & Co in 1884.
TANA LAWN *Used on the Basic Cushions (pages 14–19)*

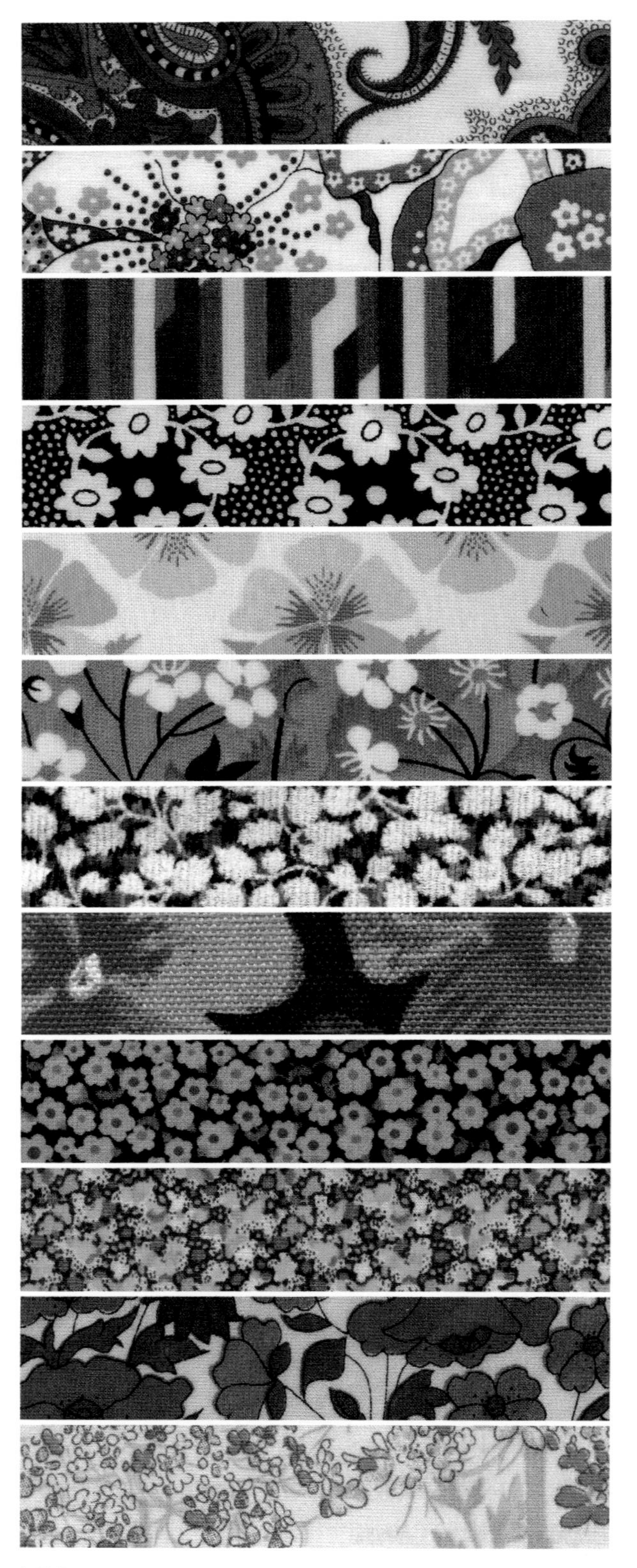

Lord Paisley is an intricate ornamental paisley based on a beautiful traditional Liberty silk scarf printed in the late 1950s.
TANA LAWN *Used on the Basic Cushions (pages 14–19)*

Mauvey was designed by the Liberty Design Studio for the spring/summer 2008 season. Based on sequinned, embroidered mallow flowers, it became part of the Classic Tana Lawn collection in 2010.
TANA LAWN *Used on the Contemporary Brick Quilt (pages 134–39)*

Mike is inspired by Pop Art and the geometric patterns used by Yves Saint Laurent throughout the 1960s.
ROSSMORE CORD *Used on the Sugar-bag Doorstop (pages 36–39)*

Millie is a check formed by small floral circles. Adapted from a bought-in old document, Liberty first produced it for the autumn/winter 2002 season. It was introduced into the Classic Tana Lawn range for 2006.
TANA LAWN *Used on the Tote Bag (pages 52–57)*

Miranda was inspired by a design from the Liberty archive. It was first printed for the spring/summer 2004 season and introduced on Tana Lawn for autumn/winter 2006.
TANA LAWN *Used on the Lampshade – Taking it Further (page 121)*

Mitsi is based on a design created by the Liberty studio during the 1950s. It plays on Liberty's history with its Japanese-style cherry blossom.
TANA LAWN *Used on the Round Cushion (pages 88–91) and Book Covers (pages 82–85)*

Pablo Pepper is a layering of two classic Liberty designs, the textured allover pattern 'Pepper' and the small leafy pattern 'Glenjade'.
ROSSMORE CORD *Used on the Beanbag (pages 48–51)*

Pansies was designed for autumn/winter 2009. The beautiful watercolour pansies design was part of a group of hand-painted designs in that season's collection.
COTTON CANVAS *Used on the Bench Cushion (pages 102–105)*

Penny was designed for autumn/winter 2011. It is based on a 1962 design in the Liberty archive.
TANA LAWN AND ROSSMORE CORD *Used on the Rose Corsage (pages 92–95) and Drawstring Bag (pages 68–71)*

Pepper was designed by the Jack Prince Studio in 1974, who designed for Liberty for many years. It has been on Classic Tana Lawn since 1979.
TANA LAWN *Used on the Rose Cushion (pages 96–101), Peacock Pincushion (pages 76–81) and Traditional Cot Quilt (pages 128–33)*

Poppy & Daisy is a stylised floral design that has been in and out of the Liberty Tana Lawn range since the early 1900s, most recently being reintroduced in 2004.
TANA LAWN *Used on the Contemporary Brick Quilt (pages 134–39)*

Princess Emerald is by the artist Michael Angove, who was commissioned specially for spring/summer 2011 to draw this lovely cow parsley pattern.
TANA LAWN *Used on the Keepsake Board – Taking It Further (page 63)*

Rania was designed for the spring/summer 2011 season. The dense scattered stars were taken from the classic Liberty design 'Mark'.
TANA LAWN *Used on the Traditional Cot Quilt (pages 128–33)*

Rock and Roll Rachel is in the autumn/winter 2011 collection. It is a rescaled version of a mid-nineteenth-century paisley shawl design in the Liberty archive.
TANA LAWN *Used on the Rose Cushion (pages 96–101)*

Rueben Kelly is a design from illustrator and painter, David McKee, who created the classic children's character Mr Benn. This flowing stripe design was based on an illustration of Mr Benn as a Liberty Print Knight.
TANA LAWN *Used on the Round Cushion (pages 88–91)*

Rumble is based on a design for Liberty's 1965 couture range.
COTTON CANVAS *Used on the Tote Bag (pages 52–57)*

Sarah's Secret Garden was inspired by the dense flowers of a Mediterranean garden.
TANA LAWN *Used on the Traditional Cot Quilt (pages 128–33)*

Sheona was designed for the spring/summer 2011 season. It is based on stars and constellations.
TANA LAWN *Used on the Washbag (pages 52–57)*

Tatum was first produced on Tana in 1955 and was derived from the 1930s Tana designs.
TANA LAWN *Used on the Traditional Cot Quilt (pages 128–33)*

Toria is inspired by the wood carvings and plaster work in and around Tudor House, Liberty's flagship store. Designed by Liberty in 2003, it was introduced on Tana Lawn in 2006.
TANA LAWN *Used on the Rose Corsage (pages 92–95)*

Viviana was specially commissioned from the watercolour artist Clare Robinson for the spring/summer 2011 season.
TANA LAWN *Used on the Simple Curtain (pages 20–23)*

Vonetta is an original design by artist and musician John Squire, formerly of the band Stone Roses. It was designed for the fall/winter 2011 season.
TANA LAWN *Used on the Basic Cushions (pages 14–19)*

Willow's Garden was designed for the spring/summer 2011 season. The daisy design is inspired by the Arts & Crafts movement.
TANA LAWN *Used on the Book Covers (pages 82–85)*

Wiltshire is a leaf and berry pattern first designed for Liberty in 1933 and updated in 1968.
TANA LAWN *Used on the Gadget Case (pages 72–75) and Rose Cushion (pages 96–101)*

Creating the first *Liberty Home Sewing Book* has been an immense pleasure. My sincere thanks to the inspirational and creative team at Liberty Art Fabrics and all those involved in this project: to Jane O'Shea, Claire Peters and Lisa Pendreigh at Quadrille Publishing, and especially to Lucinda Ganderton for her wonderful creativity.

Kirstie Carey
Managing Director
LIBERTY ART FABRICS

LIBERTY
Great Marlborough Street
London W1B 5AH
www.liberty.co.uk

Liberty fabrics are available to buy both instore and online.

Publishing Director *Jane O'Shea*
Art Director *Helen Lewis*
Project Editor *Lisa Pendreigh*
Editorial Assistant *Louise McKeever*
Project Designer and Sewing Consultant *Lucinda Ganderton*
Pattern Checker *Sally Harding*
Designer *Claire Peters*
Photographer *Kristin Perers*
Stylist *Lorraine Dawkins*
Illustrator *Richard Merritt*
Production Director *Vincent Smith*
Production Controller *James Finan*

First published in 2011 by
Quadrille Publishing Ltd
Alhambra House
27–31 Charing Cross Road
London WC2H 0LS
www.quadrille.co.uk

Reprinted in 2012
10 9 8 7 6 5 4 3 2

The props featured in this book were supplied by Liberty except those listed below:
Page 25, dress by Etro, for Liberty / Page 89, square cushion by Emma Burton, www.emmaburton.co.uk / Page 106, dress by Erdem, for Liberty / Page 134, dress by Etro, for Liberty.

British Library Cataloguing-in-Publication Data
A catalogue record for this book is available from the British Library.

ISBN: 978-184400-976-3

Printed in China